UNPRECEDENTED STEP-BY-STEP REAL ESTATE GUIDE

For Buyers, Sellers, Real Estate Professionals
FROM BEGINNER TO ADVANCED

M E Whalen

Copyright © 2025
Author Name: M E Whalen

ISBN (Paperback): 978-1-964467-93-1

ISBN (Hardcover): 978-1-964467-94-8

Contents

Dedication

To my husband, my rock, and my unwavering partner. Your service to our country and our community through 34 years in law enforcement is a testament to your strength and dedication. But even more, your love and support have been the foundation upon which this book was built. You may not have written the words, but you were there every step of the way, offering encouragement, honest feedback, and a love that kept me going, even when Chapter One seemed insurmountable. This book is as much yours as it is mine.

Acknowledgment

About 10 years ago, I read the first copy of a book written by

Donald Miller. It was a tremendous book and a great motivational

Tool. As I began writing my first book, I searched for Donald

Miller, the Author, discovered he had published a second book

in 2025. Donald, although we're not friends, your books were

my most important research in accomplish my goals.

Thank you!

Disclaimer

"Jontra is UNPRECEDENTED: Step-by-Step Real Estate Guide" is for educational and informational purposes only. It does not constitute legal, financial, or professional advice. Readers should consult with licensed professionals, including attorneys, real estate Agents, and financial advisors, before making any real estate decisions.

The author and publisher have made every effort to ensure the accuracy of the information presented. However, laws, market conditions, and financial regulations change frequently, and the information in this book may become outdated. The author and publisher assume no responsibility for any errors, omissions, or outcomes related to the use of this guide.

By reading this book, you acknowledge that any actions taken based on its contents are at your own risk. The author and publisher shall not be liable for any direct, indirect, or consequential damages resulting from the use or misuse of the information provided.

Real estate investing involves risks, and success is not guaranteed. Past performance is not indicative of future results. Readers are encouraged to conduct their due diligence and seek professional guidance before making any investment or real estate-related decisions.

By continuing to read and use this book, you agree to these terms.

Skills to Navigate Market Changes for Success

- Proven techniques are shared; all succeed.
- Engaging insights and actionable strategies—for your benefit!
- Collaborative approaches for a fair and transparent market will be successful!
- Transforming the real estate landscape when looking to buy, sell, or guide others.

In a world where the real estate landscape is transforming before our very eyes, the journey to homeownership can feel overwhelming yet exhilarating. Picture a determined Buyer, ready to take the next step toward their dream home but facing a sea of regulations and changing market norms. Enter the trusted real estate professional— armed with knowledge, empathy, and a commitment to advocacy.

Together, they embark on a quest, navigating the complexities of transactions empowered by a fundamental understanding of their rights and responsibilities.

As they traverse through insightful chapters filled with real-life stories, strategic negotiations, and the latest industry changes, readers will uncover the secrets to success in real estate. They will learn how to harness transparent practices born from the revolutionary *Settlement*, paving the way for a new era of home buying and selling. With actionable guidance and engaging narratives, this book becomes a vital companion for Buyers, sellers, and real estate professionals alike, creating pathways to opportunity and collaboration within a vibrant marketplace.

Join us on this journey, as we illuminate the path to making informed decisions, building lasting relationships, and embracing the transformations that shape the future of real estate. Your dream home awaits—let's unlock the door together.

Foreword

Important Note:

While many contracts, disclosures, and documents in this book accurately describe permanent changes to the real estate industry, copies of these documents are not included. State associations and local boards create and maintain these materials, so as a reader, please verify the source of all referenced documents from a local or state association.

For legal reasons, the name of the National Association of Real Estate and its associated terminology cannot be used. Please note the following:

- *The National Association refers to The National Association of Realtors*
- *Defendant refers to The National Association in the Legal Case*
- *Compensation refers to Commission or payment in transactions*
- *The Revolutionary Plaintiffs refers to those who initiated the legal case against the National Association.*

If confused by other "terms, please review the "Appendix or ask a real estate professional for assistance.

Introduction

As the sun rose over the picturesque town of Willow Creek in 2025, the real estate market was undergoing a dramatic transformation. Sarah and Tom, a young couple expecting their first child had spent months searching for their ideal home. They longed for a sanctuary—a place to plant roots and build lasting memories. Yet the journey had proven overwhelming, made even more complex by the recent *Revolutionary Plaintiffs Settlement*, which ushered in sweeping reforms to real estate practices across the country.

2025 Home Price Forecasts
Percent Appreciation as of 8/27/2024

Average of All 10	Goldman Sachs	Wells Fargo	HPES	Fannie Mae	Morgan Stanley	MBA	Zelman & Associates	NAR	Freddie Mac	Moody's Analytics
2.6	4.4	4.3	3.2	3.0	3.0	2.9	2.3	1.9	0.6	0.3

Meanwhile, Emily, a dedicated real estate Agent with years of experience, prepared herself for a busy day. She was acutely aware of the newfound pressure on all parties involved. Buyers were more informed than ever, Sellers were adjusting to new compensation structures, and real estate professionals like her needed to adapt quickly to this evolving landscape. As she prepared her Client presentations and strategized marketing

ix

techniques, Emily understood that knowledge and transparency were no longer luxuries—they were essential.

Across town, seasoned Seller Lisa faced unexpected challenges. New disclosure requirements introduced by the Settlement obligated her to provide extensive details—not just about the home's condition and repairs but also the character of the neighborhood. With Buyers more cautious and better educated, Lisa questioned whether she could find a real estate professional who could truly guide her through this unfamiliar terrain.

Later that day, Sarah and Tom walked into an open house and were greeted by Emily. She immediately recognized their hesitation. In this post-settlement market, Buyers had gained greater negotiating power and were demanding more from their Agents—clarity, communication, and advocacy. Emily, aware of the growing expectations, took this opportunity to reassure them, emphasizing how her role was not just to sell a house, but to *empower them throughout the entire process.*

In today's real estate environment, every decision—by Buyers, Sellers, and professionals—is deeply interconnected. The journey has become a complex dance of negotiation, understanding, and collaboration—where success hinges on a solid grasp of the new norms. *This book is designed to equip you with the tools, insights, and strategies you need to navigate this transformed landscape, whether you're looking to buy, sell, or guide others along their path*

Chapter 1

We begin with a landmark case and the Revolutionary Plaintiffs who challenged key problems, sparking widespread changes in real estate practices.

A Turning Point in Real Estate

Real change in real estate often begins behind closed doors—in courtrooms, in boardrooms—and gradually reshapes the way homes are bought and sold across the country. In November 2024, a groundbreaking $418 million settlement in the case of *Revolutionary Plaintiffs v. The National Association* sent shockwaves through the industry. What started with a small group of Missouri home Sellers evolved into a nationwide reckoning with outdated practices that had long burdened consumers and stifled competition.

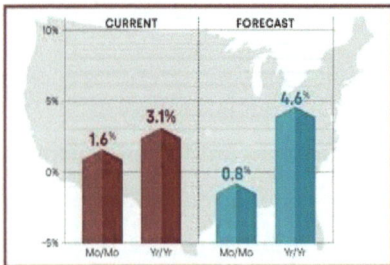

These Plaintiffs challenged what they saw as a system that inflated costs and limited choice. At the heart of the dispute was the traditional commission-sharing model, a long-standing structure where Listing Agents offered predetermined compensation to Buyers' Agents through the Multiple Listing Service (MLS). The Plaintiffs argued that this practice unfairly locked Sellers into paying inflated fees—regardless of the actual value delivered by the Buyer's Agent.

1

Their legal complaints highlighted several core issues:

- **High Commission Rates**: The Plaintiffs argued that these rules enforced artificial and non-negotiable commission rates, which hampered Sellers by inflating their overall costs.

- **MLS System Manipulation**: They contended that the National Association's Multiple Listing Service (MLS) facilitated anti-competitive practices, restricting transparent negotiations on commissions, thereby dictating how commissions were split between Agents.

- **Buyer Agent Incentives**: The Revolutionary Plaintiffs complained that the structure incentivized Buyer Agents to steer their Clients toward homes with higher compensation, potentially compromising the true interests of Buyers.

- **Code of Ethics Enforcement**: Lastly, they asserted that the National Association's Code of Ethics was misused, preventing Brokers from openly negotiating commission rates with Sellers.

Together, these practices created barriers to fair representation, increasing costs and undermining consumer trust.

Yet, this legal dispute was more than a singular event; it was part of a larger narrative challenging the very foundation of what was referred to as the traditional compensation model in real estate. The lawsuits illuminated long-standing practices upheld by the National Association, revealing the complexities and costs involved in the home-selling process.

As news of the Settlement spread, real estate professionals across the country—Agents, Brokers, and legal experts—scrambled to interpret its implications. While the National Association insisted its rules promoted market-driven pricing, the reality on the ground told a different story. Concerns about uncertainty loomed large as real estate professionals grappled with the implications of this seismic shift. Out of the uncertainty, however, came opportunity.

The Settlement ushered in an era of transparency and empowerment for Buyers and Sellers alike. Increased awareness of rights and responsibilities, along with updated disclosure requirements, created a level playing field where ethical representation flourished. For Sellers and Buyers in communities like Willow Creek, these new regulations weren't just bureaucratic changes—they symbolized a commitment to fairness and integrity in the marketplace. Armed with clear compensation structures and transparent practices, Clients could engage with their real estate professionals confidently, making informed decisions about their transactions.

This book serves as a comprehensive step-by-step guide and resource, delving deep into the crucial changes within the real estate industry. Here, you will explore not only the facts and figures but also the inspiring stories of those who have fought for fairness and transparency. Join us as we navigate the ramifications of the Revolutionary Plaintiffs' case, uncovering the journey toward an equitable real estate market where new opportunities await, and empowered Buyers or Sellers are ready to embrace their dreams of homeownership.

What Happened? A Revolution Occurred

In the ever-evolving landscape of real estate, a significant revolution unfolded fueled by consumer demand for fairness and transparency. The real estate industry faced scrutiny as far as concerned *Buyers and Sellers accused it of operating in outdated ways*, leading to misconceptions about compliance with modern laws.

Recognizing the need for reform, a wave of change swept through the industry, mandating new legal requirements that would reshape the market forever.

The Catalyst for Change: The Settlement

The turning point came with the landmark "Settlement," finalized on November 26, 2024. This transformative legal shift mandated greater transparency in compensation and disclosure practices, *forever altering the fabric of real estate transactions*. The Settlement aimed to create an equitable environment where consumers had increased choices and clarity about the costs associated with buying and selling homes.

Gone were the days of hidden fees and ambiguous compensation structures. The Settlement directly addressed the outdated practices that had restricted consumer options, allowing Buyers and Sellers alike to navigate the market with confidence. Real estate professionals also adapted to this new system, prioritizing clarity and ethical practices in every transaction.

Negotiation: YOUR Vital Skill for Success

In this new market landscape, negotiation emerged as a critical skill for success. For Buyer's and Seller's Agents, mastering the nuances of negotiation meant leveraging market insights to achieve their goals. They learned that effective communication, understanding motivations, and exploring creative solutions could turn challenges into opportunities.

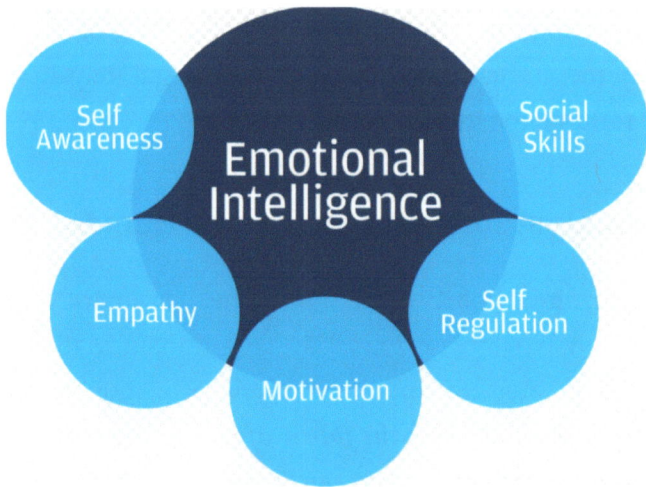

For real estate professionals, strong negotiation skills are the element to delivering service and securing the best outcomes for their Buyer or Seller. As these professionals refined their approach, they came to understand that negotiation extends far beyond price. It involves managing relationships, navigating emotions, and above all, building trust- a vital asset in the post-Settlement era where transparency and Client empowerment are at the forefront.

Success: Realizing the Dream of Homeownership

Amid all these changes, one thing remained constant: real estate professionals retained the power to help their Clients achieve the dream of homeownership. With comprehensive step-by-step instructions (which you receive in this book) provided, both Buyer and Seller will confidently rely on their real estate professional for guidance. *The overarching goal is to uphold "The Truth, The Whole Truth, and Nothing but the Truth" in every transaction.*

Court Grants Final Agreement of the Settlement

On November 26, 2024, the court granted final approval of the "Settlement." Judge Bough of the U.S. District Court for the Western District of Missouri heard from all parties involved, including objectors and the Department of Justice (DOJ).

Real Estate: A Journey through Change

In the quaint, bustling town of Willow Creek, where the past meets the present, a young couple named Emily and Jason stood at the threshold of their first home. Excitement bubbled in their hearts as they envisioned a future filled with laughter and love. Yet, as they prepared for this monumental journey, they acknowledged that understanding the real estate market was essential for making informed decisions.

"Did you know that real estate has evolved dramatically over the centuries?" Emily asked, curious about the history behind their journey. "I wonder how it all began."

Jason smiled. "Well, it started back in the colonial days, when transactions were informal—a handshake could seal the deal. They relied on communication and mutual agreements rather than structured systems."

As they strolled down the tree-lined streets, they pictured early settlers negotiating land without contracts, relying instead on word of mouth and good faith. "It wasn't until major events—like the Homestead Act—that property ownership took on new meaning," Jason continued. "That's when land began to be distributed in a more organized way, and structured property transactions became the norm."

Their discussion wandered into the complexities of today's market dynamics. "With supply and demand constantly shifting, it's fascinating to think about how economic factors like interest rates and job growth influence property values," Emily remarked, contemplating the landscape before them.

"And now," Jason added, "real estate professionals are held to strict ethical standards. Organizations like the National Association ensure both Buyer and Seller Agents work with integrity, loyalty, and confidentiality."

As they approached a Listing sign, Emily noted how organized real estate had become. "It's remarkable how far we've come since those early days," she said. "The introduction of the Code of Ethics in 1913 was a significant step toward professionalism. It helps today's Agents navigate their responsibilities and prioritize Client protection."

Jason nodded in agreement and began to elaborate on the CLIENT principles embedded in the Code of Ethics:

- Confidentiality: Maintaining Client information as private.

- Loyalty: Putting the Client's needs above all else.

- Integrity: Acting with honest and ethical behavior.

- Expertise: Maintaining professional knowledge and competence.

- Notice: Disclosing all material facts about a property.

- Treatment of all parties fairly: Treating everyone involved in a transaction with respect and fairness.

As they stood beneath the Listing sign, Jason added, "Over time, advancements like standardized forms and professional guidelines made transactions clearer and more efficient. However, for many years, critical elements like compensation structure and property listing practices were rarely discussed openly."

Emily smiled, intrigued. It was fascinating to imagine how early real estate professionals managed their work, perhaps with little more than handwritten notes and in-person meetings. Jason chuckled. "Can you imagine? The invention of the telephone in 1876 must've revolutionized things. Still, I wonder how long it took before Agents used it for business."

One thing was certain: with the establishment of the Code of Ethics, the real estate industry took its first major step toward professionalism and accountability. As they looked toward their future in this quickly evolving market, Emily and Jason felt reassured. They understood that not only were they participating in a transaction of financial significance, but they were also engaging in a system that recognized the importance of ethical standards and Client protection.

This book will explore the rich history of real estate, the transformative changes shaping today's market, and the core principles guiding real estate professionals. Join us as we delve into a world where knowledge meets practical application, empowering you with the insights needed to navigate your real estate journey with confidence.

A New Era in Real Estate: The $418 Million Turning Point

In the world of real estate, the $418 million Settlement agreement was finalized on November 26, 2024. The Revolutionary Plaintiffs v. the National Association case was a pivotal moment, echoing through the industry like a thunderclap. It all began with a group of angry home Sellers from Missouri who decided to confront what they believed was an outdated and unfair system that inflated their costs.

These Sellers, now known as the Revolutionary Plaintiffs, took a stand against what they saw as an outdated and unfair system—one that inflated their costs and restricted their choices. As the legal battle unfolded, their frustrations became clear: the longstanding compensation-sharing rules between Listing and Buyer Agents had, in their view, locked Sellers into a cycle of excessive expenses.

The key complaints brought forward in the case included:

- *High Compensation Rates*: The Revolutionary Plaintiffs argued that the National Association's rules led to artificially inflated and non-negotiable compensation rates, specifically requiring Sellers to pay compensation to Buyer Agents. Revolutionary Plaintiffs referenced this practice ultimately hurt Sellers by increasing their overall costs.

- *MLS System Manipulation*: The Revolutionary Plaintiffs claimed that policies influenced by the National Association and implemented across many MLS platforms facilitated anti-competitive practices. Specifically, they argued that these practices restricted transparent negotiations overcompensation and effectively dictated how commissions were shared between Buyer and Listing Agents—limiting Sellers' ability to negotiate fees freely.

- *Buyer's Agent Incentives*: The Revolutionary Plaintiffs argued that the system incentivized Buyer Agents to steer Clients toward homes that offered higher compensation, potentially compromising the best interests of Agents.

- *Code of Ethics Enforcement*: Lastly, they contended that the National Association's Code of Ethics was misused to enforce these practices, hindering Broker from openly negotiating compensation rates with Sellers.

  These rules created barriers that made home selling not just a transaction but a costly battle against unseen forces.

The Revolutionary Plaintiff's case was not just one legal dispute; it is part of a larger narrative challenging the very foundation of the traditional real estate compensation model. Alongside the other cases, these lawsuits shine a light on long-standing practices enforced by the National Association, revealing the complexities and costs involved in the home-selling Buyer's process.

As news of the Settlement spread, the real estate industry braced for impact. The National Association maintained that its rules encouraged market-driven pricing and competition that ultimately benefited consumers. However, many real estate professionals and Brokers on the ground felt differently. The reality they faced was marked by uncertainty, as they grappled with the implications of this seismic shift and what it would mean for their roles, their Clients, and the future of real estate as a whole.

Yet, as the dust began to settle, a new beginning emerged in the real estate landscape. The Settlement fostered an era of transparency and empowerment for Buyers and Sellers. Increased awareness of rights and responsibilities, along with updated disclosure requirements, created a level playing field where ethical representation was paramount.

For Sellers and Buyers in communities like Willow Creek, the new regulations were not simply bureaucratic changes; they symbolized a commitment to fairness in the marketplace. Armed with clear compensation structures and transparent practices, Clients could engage with real estate professionals confidently, making informed decisions about their transactions.

This book delves deep into these crucial changes in the real estate sector, exploring the facts and figures and the stories of those who have fought for fairness and transparency. Join us and navigate through the ramifications of the Revolutionary Plaintiffs case and discover the journey toward a more equitable real estate market, where new opportunities await, and empowered Clients can embrace their dreams of homeownership.

Chapter 2

Real Estate and the Economy
Misconceptions about Compliance with Modern Laws

Market Trends, Legal impacts, and dealing with the Economy: Roles in Real Estate

Market Trends and Their Impact on Real Estate

The real estate market is dynamic, characterized by cyclical behavior influenced by the balance of supply and demand. Understanding these trends is essential for all stakeholders to navigate this ever-changing landscape effectively.

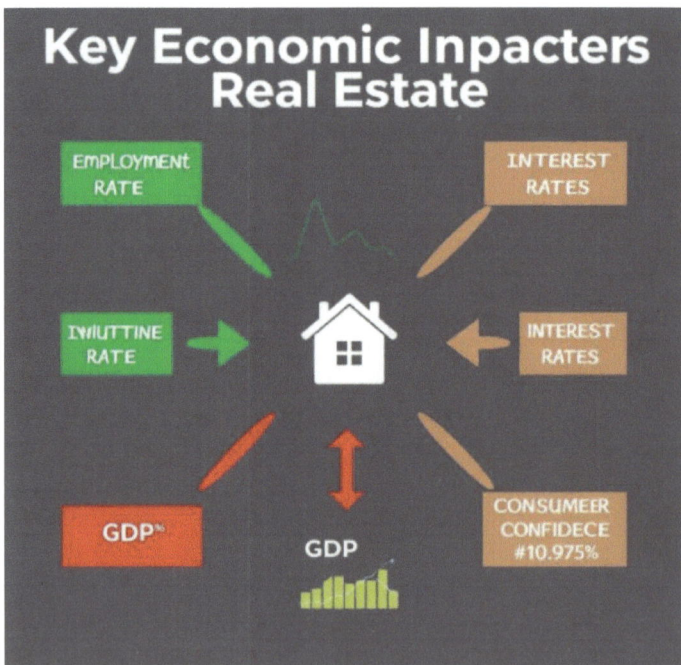

Seller Market

In a Seller's market, high demand and limited inventory create competitive bidding environments, often driving prices upward. These conditions typically arise during periods of economic growth and low unemployment, when consumer confidence is high. In such environments, real estate professionals must guide Clients on strategic bidding, competitive offers, and fast-paced negotiations to secure optimal results.

Buyer Market

A real estate Buyer's market occurs when the supply of available properties exceeds the demand from Buyers. This often leads to lower prices and more negotiating power for Buyers, as Sellers may need to make concessions to attract offers. In such a market, Buyers can access a greater variety of options and potentially secure better deals.

Neutral Market

Conversely, a neutral market reflects a balanced supply and demand relationship, allowing for smoother transactions and stable pricing. Buyers and Sellers can find common ground in negotiations, leading to positive experiences for all involved. Here, comprehensive market analyses become essential tools for guiding Client expectations.

Technological Disruption in Real Estate

Innovation is rapidly transforming the industry. Advances in property technology (PropTech), including virtual reality (VR) tours, artificial intelligence (AI), and automation, are streamlining property exploration and decision-making processes. AI-powered tools provide market insights in real time, enabling professionals to adapt strategies swiftly and stay ahead of emerging trends.

Practical Takeaways for Real Estate Professionals

Real estate professionals should implement the following strategies:

- **Monitor Economic Indicators**: Stay updated on key economic indicators like employment rates, inflation, and interest rates, as these factors directly influence market conditions and Client decisions.
- **Educate Clients**: Provide Clients with clear, comprehensive information on how economic factors affect their timing and budget. Empowering Clients leads to informed decisions.
- **Adapt Strategies**: In challenging market conditions, explore creative financing options and consider alternative property types. Flexibility can lead to new opportunities, ensuring successful transactions.

The Landscape of Real Estate:
A Tale of Change and Connection

In the vibrant town of Willow Creek, the real estate market was buzzing with energy, drawing in Buyers and Sellers from all walks of life. It was a landscape rich with opportunity, yet complex and ever-changing, shaped by the ebb and flow of economic currents.

For real estate professional Emily, this dynamic environment meant every day brought new challenges and opportunities to navigate.

On a crisp autumn morning, Emily prepared for a packed schedule. Not long ago, she hosted a community workshop discussing the landmark Revolutionary Plaintiffs v. The National Association Settlement. The conversation sparked deep interest among locals, many of whom were navigating the Buying or Selling process in real time.

As she settled at her desk, Emily reflected on how much the industry had transformed. Greater transparency, a new compensation structure, and an increased emphasis on ethics had reshaped how Agents operated. What once felt rigid and transactional now demanded adaptability, communication, and care.

- **Future Outlook:** As the real estate landscape continues to evolve, several technological advancements and shifting consumer priorities will shape its trajectory. Understanding these trends is essential for real estate professionals:

- **AI-Driven Transactions**: Artificial intelligence is expected to streamline processes and enhance the buying and selling experience. With AI tools reducing transaction times, professionals must adapt while ensuring consumer data protection.

- **Sustainability Mandates**: Growing environmental concerns will increasingly influence the market, with regulations promoting energy-efficient upgrades and eco-friendly developments.

- **Growth in Secondary Markets**: As urban living becomes more expensive, smaller cities and affordable regions are rising in popularity, offering opportunities for real estate professionals to tap into emerging markets.

The Legal Landscape of Real Estate: A Journey Through Structure and Rights:

In the world of real estate, a complex web of laws, regulations, and practices serves as the backbone for every property transaction. This legal framework is more than mere rules; it embodies fairness, protects ownership rights, and structures the intricate dance of property ownership and transfer. However, navigating this landscape is essential for all participants in the market.

- **The Case of the Revolutionary Plaintiffs:** Our tale begins with a landmark case known as the Revolutionary Plaintiffs, which emerged from the shadows of allegations regarding anti-competitive practices woven into compensation structures within the industry. This was no ordinary legal battle; it was steeped in antitrust laws and reflected a broader movement toward fairness and accountability in real estate dealings. The resolution of this case sets the stage for a transformative shift in how real estate transactions are conducted.

- **A New Dawn: Implications of the Settlement:** As the dust settled from the Revolutionary Plaintiffs Settlement, a new era dawned upon the real estate industry. The Settlement ushered in a wave of greater transparency and competitive pricing in compensation. Professionals within the field quickly realized that adaptability was no longer optional; innovation and a Client-focused approach became the keys to thriving in this evolving landscape.

- **The Transformation of Commission Structures:** Gone were the days of rigid compensation offers. The real estate sector witnessed a dramatic shift, where Buyers and Sellers were now empowered to negotiate directly. This newfound power placed greater responsibility on professionals, encouraging and assisting them to rethink their strategies and embrace a more collaborative dynamic.

- **Gazing into the Future, Trends in Real Estate Law:** Looking ahead, the horizon of real estate law reveals promising trends. There is an increasing emphasis on consumer protection, enhanced transparency, and the integration of technology. As these regulations evolve, the professionals in the field must stay vigilant, continuously educating themselves to remain compliant and successful in their endeavors.

- **Exploring the Varieties of Real Estate:** The varieties you will find in real estate are not a monolith; it is a vibrant tapestry woven from various types, including residential, commercial, industrial, and agricultural properties. Each category holds its unique purpose—housing families, facilitating businesses, enabling manufacturing, and fostering agriculture. Understanding these distinctions equips stakeholders to navigate the myriad opportunities and challenges presented within each sector.

- **The Heartbeat of Property, Valuation, and Transactions:** Valuation serves as the heartbeat of the real estate realm, determining a property's worth through a plethora of factors such as the state of the economy, market trends, desirable locations, and comparable sales. Transactions, the lifeblood of the industry, involve the meticulous transfer of ownership or rights. This intricate process requires a harmonious blend of accurate valuation and legal adherence.

- **The Laws that Govern:** Real estate law is a vast domain that encompasses zoning regulations, environmental statutes, landlord-tenant rules, and fair housing policies. These laws, which can vary significantly from one jurisdiction to another, profoundly influence property development, usage, and sales. Real estate professionals must remain informed, adapting to the ever-changing legal landscape.

- **Understanding Property Rights:** At the core of real estate law are property rights, which delineate how land and structures can be owned, used, and transferred. These rights include possession, control, exclusion, and disposition—forming the bedrock of property law that empowers owners to utilize their assets within the bounds of legality.

- **Guiding Lights, The Role of Real Estate Professionals:** In this intricate world, real estate professionals serve as vital guides for Buyers, Sellers, and Investors. With their expertise in valuation, marketing, negotiations, and legal requirements, they navigate.

The complexities of the market ensure that transactions are not only successful but also compliant.

- **A Tale of Two Roles: Agents vs. Brokers:** Within the realm of real estate, Agents and Brokers play distinct yet complementary roles. Seller Agents acts as intermediaries, facilitating transactions with Buyer and

Seller, while Brokers, equipped with advanced credentials, oversee these transactions often managing teams of Agents. Understanding this dynamic is crucial for fostering collaboration in the industry.

- **Upholding Ethics: Standards in Real Estate:** Amidst the transactions and negotiations, ethical standards emerge as a cornerstone of the real estate profession. These guiding principles promote integrity, fairness, and professionalism, shaping how practitioners engage with Clients, disclose information, and conduct transactions — all essential for building trust and protecting the interests of all parties involved.

- **Contracts, The Framework of Agreements:** Contracts stand at the forefront of real estate transactions, serving as legally binding agreements that link parties to specific terms. Detailed and precise, these agreements outline responsibilities, timelines, and contingencies, providing a clear framework for managing expectations and resolving disputes effectively.

- **Navigating Common Legal Waters:** Every journey in real estate can encounter turbulent waters, often marked by common legal issues such as boundary disputes, zoning challenges, title defects, and breaches of contract.

It is clear that the real estate industry is more than just a marketplace; it's a cornerstone of opportunity, innovation, and transformation. By understanding the intricate web of legal frameworks, adapting to technological advancements, and navigating shifting compensation structures, professionals will thrive in this field.

As you apply this knowledge, remember that the heart of real estate lies in relationships—building trust, serving Clients, and adapting to their needs. By embracing these insights and applying them thoughtfully, you are poised to navigate challenges, seize opportunities, and lead with integrity in an ever-evolving industry.

In the Market, Understanding Individual Needs

From this perspective, Emily thought back to her first meeting with Julie. They had met in a cozy local coffee shop, where the aroma of freshly brewed coffee mingled with soft conversation.

"What are your goals?" Emily asked gently, encouraging openness.

Julie smiled, then shared her dream: a home with enough space for her growing family and a backyard where her children could play.

As they discussed budget constraints and preferences, Emily made it a point to break down Julie's goals into primary and secondary objectives. Knowing what truly mattered would guide their search for the right property.

Meanwhile, across town, Mark, a Seller eager to move to a new city, was contemplating how best to price his property in light of recent market trends. He had learned from friends that the current market was competitive, yet he felt unsure of how to position his home effectively.

Enter Lisa, his real estate Seller's Agent and a seasoned professional who understood the nuances of market conditions.

"Let's analyze the recent sales in your area, factoring in the latest comparable listings," Lisa suggested as they reviewed relevant data. Mark felt reassured by her expertise, recognizing the importance of aligning his strategy with current market conditions to attract the right Buyer.

As real estate transactions unfolded in Willow Creek, the influence of economic indicators, such as employment rates and consumer confidence, became more apparent. Emily, a Buyer, observed how these factors swayed negotiations as Buyers sought to secure the best deals.

Real Estate is a dynamic and multifaceted industry, intricately woven into the fabric of our economy, communities, and daily lives. Whether you are Buying, Selling, Investing, or guiding Clients through the process, understanding the diverse elements of real estate is essential for success.

This resource brings together key concepts and contemporary insights—from foundational principles like property rights and valuation to the evolving impact of law, technology, and ethics.

As you explore various types of real estate, unpack legal frameworks, or navigate the changes brought about by the Revolutionary Plaintiffs v. the National Association, this guide is designed to empower you with knowledge and practical insights.

The Art of Negotiation: Negotiation is an art, and it requires understanding individual personalities. Emily often identified key traits in her Clients; for instance, Julie tended to lean towards emotional decision-making, drawn to the aesthetics and feel of a home. In contrast, Mark was more rational and results-driven, focused on maximizing his return.

To illustrate the power of understanding personalities, Emily recalled a negotiation session where Julie hesitated to make an offer on a home that felt perfect but was slightly above her budget. Emily encouraged her, inviting Julie to consider her non-negotiable aspects, such as the home's location and amenities.

"Let's think strategically," Emily proposed. "If we present a compelling offer below the list price and highlight your eagerness as a first-time Buyer, we might attract the Seller's attention. They want to feel confident about their choice too." This collaborative approach reassured Julie, who felt empowered by the support of her Agent.

As negotiations progressed, both Buyers and Sellers faced the realities of the market with a new lens, informed by the landscape shifting beneath them. Mark successfully sold his home, leveraging Lisa's insights on pricing strategy, and Julie ultimately secured her family's dream home, guided by Emily's unwavering support.

Embracing the Journey: Throughout each transaction, a common thread emerged: the economy, market trends, and individual personalities intertwined to shape outcomes. Both real estate professionals and Clients had become attuned to this intricate dance, evolving their strategies to meet the challenges they faced.

In the end, Willow Creek's real estate market stood as a testament to the resilience and adaptability of its participants. Empowered by knowledge, guided by transparency, and bolstered by strong relationships, Buyers and Sellers confidently navigated the complexities of the journey toward homeownership.

As the golden sun set beyond the horizon, illuminating the vibrant community, Emily embraced the ever-evolving world of real estate, excited for the opportunities that awaited. After all, every transaction was not just about properties but about connecting people, dreams, and aspirations in a world ripe for transformation.

Understanding the economy, market trends, and the personalities that drive market behavior is vital for successfully navigating the complexities of real estate. By remaining vigilant about economic indicators, leveraging emerging technologies, and adapting to shifting consumer preferences, real estate professionals, Buyers, and Sellers can strategically position themselves for success.

In an industry characterized by constant change, knowledge remains the most valuable tool for navigating the market landscape. Insights into individual, collective, and generational personalities provide professionals and their Clients with a deeper understanding of the "why" behind market trends. This knowledge equips them to adapt effectively to ongoing shifts and make informed decisions across various aspects, including pricing, negotiation, and marketing strategies. Ultimately, these factors contribute to not only immediate success but also sustainable growth and long-term success within the real estate market.

More Than 1 in 3 Zoomers Live with Their Parents, Along with 1 in 10 Millennials

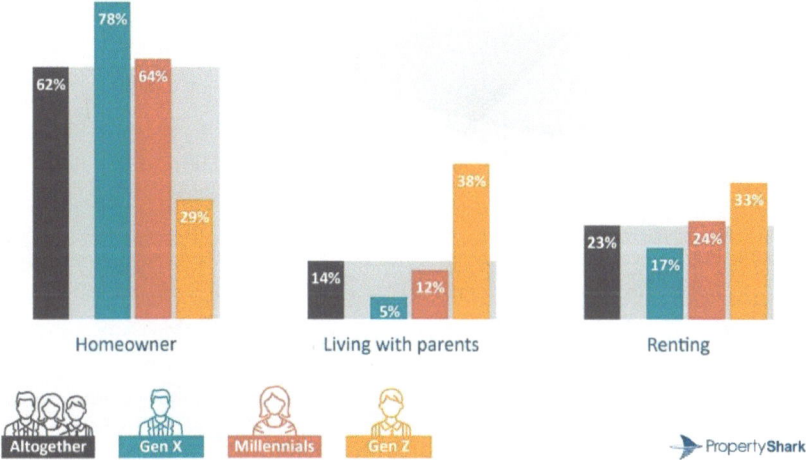

Homeowner: 62%, 78%, 64%, 29%
Living with parents: 14%, 5%, 12%, 38%
Renting: 23%, 17%, 24%, 33%

Altogether | Gen X | Millennials | Gen Z

PropertyShark

Navigating Personalities in Real Estate Transactions: As the sun began to rise over Willow Creek, casting a warm glow across the landscape, Emily prepared for an informative meeting with her Clients—Mark and Lisa, a couple eager to sell their home. They had heard whispers of changing market dynamics and strategies for negotiating effectively, and Emily was ready to guide them through the complexities of their real estate journey.

Understanding Individual Personalities: Emily started the conversation by emphasizing the importance of understanding the psychological aspects of both Buyers and Sellers. "Navigating this market means recognizing how different personalities influence our interactions," she explained, leaning in to capture their attention.

"Take risk tolerance, for example," Emily continued. "It varies widely among individuals. Some Sellers might be adventurous and willing to invest in emerging markets, while others, like yourselves, may prefer stable neighborhoods with established values. Recognizing where you stand on this spectrum will help us tailor our approach."

Mark and Lisa nodded, eager to align their objectives with Emily's insights.

Decision-Making Dynamics: Emily introduced another critical aspect: decision-making styles. "I've noticed that Buyers often fall into two categories—emotional and practical decision-makers. Emotional Buyers, for instance, might prioritize the aesthetics and emotional appeal of a home," she explained, "while practical Buyers focus on metrics like investment potential and resale value."

Understanding this helped Emily navigate negotiations effectively, ensuring that property features aligned with her Clients' priorities.

Negotiation Styles in Action: As they shifted to discuss their negotiation strategy, Emily pointed out how different negotiation styles could impact outcomes. "Some Sellers may adopt an assertive approach, pushing for higher prices," she said, "which can lengthen the listing periods if Buyers hesitate to meet those elevated expectations. Meanwhile, flexible negotiators are often better positioned to close deals quickly, even if it involves settling for less favorable terms."

Mark and Lisa recognized the importance of flexibility in their strategy, aware now that adaptability could lead to smoother transactions.

Broader Market Dynamics: "Then there's the effect of collective market personalities," Emily said. "During housing booms, we see a phenomenon known as FOMO—fear of missing out. It drives urgency among Buyers, leading to price surges. Sellers can capitalize on this sentiment, but they must be careful not to overreach lest they miss potential opportunities."

"It's easy to get caught up in the excitement, isn't it?" Lisa remarked, reflecting on the competitive nature of the market.

Emily nodded. "Absolutely. And let's not forget about generational influences. Different generations, from Millennials to Baby Boomers, have unique preferences that shape their real estate goals. Millennials often seek walkable neighborhoods and sustainable homes, while Baby Boomers may gravitate toward family-oriented properties."

The Role of Economic Influencers: Finally, Emily touched on how external economic influencers can sway market sentiment. "Prominent economists and thought leaders have significant sway. Their analysis can inform our approach. If a respected figure predicts a downturn, we may need to adjust our strategies accordingly," she pointed out.

Mark and Lisa exchanged glances, realizing the myriad factors that impacted their decisions.

Conclusion: Empowering Growth Through Knowledge

As their meeting ended, Emily emphasized the importance of continuing education and adaptation within the real estate landscape. With a deeper understanding of individual personalities, market dynamics, and external influences, Mark and Lisa felt empowered to make informed decisions throughout their selling process.

Equipped with this knowledge, they left the meeting energized, ready to embrace the journey ahead with confidence, knowing that understanding personalities and dynamics would play a significant role in their success in the market.

Individual Buyers and Seller Personalities: In an industry characterized by constant change, knowledge remains the most valuable tool for navigating the market landscape. Insights into individual, collective, and generational personalities provide professionals and their Buyers with a deeper understanding of the "why" behind market trends. This knowledge equips them to adapt effectively to ongoing shifts and make informed decisions across various aspects, including pricing, negotiation, and marketing strategies. Ultimately, these factors contribute to not only immediate success but also sustainable growth and long-term success within the real estate market.

Chapter 3

Mastering the Modern MLS

Settlement Result: Modern MLS

MLS System – A Marketplace of Possibilities

In the bustling world of real estate, the **Multiple Listing Service (MLS)** stands as a cornerstone—a dynamic marketplace where properties come alive and connections are forged. Imagine it as a grand bazaar, filled with vibrant stalls—each representing a home, a plot of land, or an investment opportunity. Once a tool known only to insiders, the MLS has grown into the lifeblood of modern real estate transactions, linking Listing and Buyer Agents in a vast network of shared opportunities.

But what exactly is the MLS?

At its core, MLS is a comprehensive database where Listing Agent showcase their properties to Buyer's Agents, creating a network driven by collaboration and shared goals. For decades, it has operated on the principle of transparency, allowing real estate professionals to access vital information about homes for sale, including prices, features, and market histories. This sharing of data creates a competitive edge, helping the Seller match the Buyer with the dream homes more efficiently.

However, within this seemingly straightforward system lies a labyrinth of policies and practices that can confuse even the savvy participants. Traditionally, MLS has enforced a set of rules that state how compensation is shared between Listing and Buyer Agents. While these rules were designed to incentivize cooperation, they have also given rise to a series of challenges—especially for Seller.

As lawsuits like Revolutionary Plaintiffs v. the National Association and others explore, many home Sellers have found themselves caught in a web of what they refer to as *inflated costs stemming from these compensation structures*. They argue that the requirement which mandates Listing Agent to offer compensation to the Buyer Agent distorts the true value of their properties, often leading to higher selling expenses that they can ill afford.

Despite the controversies, the MLS remains an essential tool in the real estate toolkit. It democratizes access to information, levels the playing field, and empowers homeowners and Agents alike. As we delve deeper into its intricacies, we'll uncover stories of triumph and hardship, illustrating how the MLS has influenced not just the market but the very fabric of real estate transactions. Join us on this journey as we navigate through the history, structure, and implications of the MLS System, all while spotlighting the voices of those who have experienced its twists and turns firsthand. Together, we will reveal just how significant this system is in shaping the landscape of modern real estate.

A New Era in the MLS – Empowering Buyers and Sellers

In the wake of the groundbreaking Revolutionary Plaintiffs v. the National Association Settlement, the Multiple Listing Service (MLS) stands at a transformative crossroads. Gone are the days when the compensation structure dictated the flow of real estate transactions, creating a one-size-fits-all approach that often left Sellers feeling tethered and uninformed. A new chapter is unfolding—one that champions negotiation and empowers Agents, offering a fresh perspective on how Agents operate within this landscape.

Picture: a vibrant open house buzzing with energy. Potential Buyers walk through rooms that speak to their dreams and aspirations, each corner echoing with conversations about future possibilities. But now, as they navigate this journey, they do so with an unprecedented tool at their disposal—the Buyer's Agent Contract Agreement.

This innovative shift encourages Buyers to engage their real estate professionals in thoughtful negotiation, allowing them to outline their specific needs and preferences in a formalized manner. No longer are Buyers and their real estate professionals bound by rigid compensation dictates; instead, they now have the freedom to discuss fees openly and decide what works best for both parties. The very foundation of trust and collaboration is built into this new agreement, transforming how real estate professionals and Clients communicate.

As Agents step into this empowered role, they are no longer mere intermediaries—they are trusted partners in their Clients' real estate journeys. Picture an Agent who listens with intention, crafting bespoke strategies tailored to each Client's unique situation. With the Buyer's Agent Contract Agreement in place, Agents are incentivized to deliver services that go far beyond the transaction—services that resonate with the Client's dreams, goals, and financial realities.

Leading this charge are forward-thinking professionals who recognize the power of negotiation over obligation. These pioneers embrace innovative practices and openly share their success stories—motivating others in the industry to do the same. As the traditional model fades into history, these Agents are forging a new future grounded in transparency, value, and professional dignity.

But this evolution doesn't come without growing pains. While many Agents welcome the freedom and flexibility of the new landscape, others face the daunting reality of reinvention. In boardrooms and coffee shops alike, murmurs of skepticism can still be heard. Some ask: How will this affect our income? Our workflows? Our worth?

Yet, it is precisely within this uncertainty that creativity, confidence, and adaptability are born. A growing network of real estate Agents begins to champion new training programs centered around effective negotiation strategies, redefining the skill sets essential to thrive in this changing environment. Workshops unfold, sharing tactics for engaging Clients in meaningful discussions about compensations and service levels, ensuring each Agent is equipped with the tools to succeed in this new order.

As these changes take root, the MLS becomes a more dynamic and flexible platform, enhancing the market experience for both Buyers and Sellers. No longer is it merely a database of Listings; it has transformed into a powerful ecosystem where relationships flourish and collaboration thrive.

As we journey through this evolving landscape, we'll hear from Agents who have embraced their newfound agency, sharing stories of negotiations that led to remarkable value, satisfaction, and empowerment. Together, the industry navigates this new paradigm, moving toward a more equitable real estate future—one where collaboration is celebrated, and both Buyers and Sellers flourish in the process.

The New Era – Transformative Changes in the MLS

As the sun set over the charming town of Willow Creek, the air was thick with anticipation. The real estate industry had been buzzing with talk of groundbreaking changes driven by the landmark case, Revolutionary Plaintiffs v. the National Association. The recent Settlement was not merely a legal victory; it signaled a profound shift aimed at fostering fairness, transparency, and trust within the marketplace.

The Drive for Change

At the heart of these changes were the *complaints of the Revolutionary Plaintiffs, a coalition of home Sellers who united to challenge what they described as an outdated and expensive compensation structure within the real estate framework.* They believed that existing practices artificially inflated home prices and limited consumer choice, leading to unnecessary burdens on

Sellers, ultimately requiring Buyers to pay more.

The Revolutionary Plaintiffs sought redress under the Sherman Antitrust Act, arguing they believed that the cooperative compensation model enforced by the National Association violated antitrust laws by creating a monopolistic environment. This model restricted competition, stifled negotiations, and perpetuated a system that benefited Agents at the expense of consumers.

With the Settlement in place, everything was set to transform. As Sarah, a seasoned real estate Agent, convened with her colleagues at a local seminar, the atmosphere buzzed with curiosity and excitement about the implications of the new rules.

Understanding the Key Changes

As the attendees listened intently, Sarah outlined the essential elements defining the new MLS policies:

- **Compliance Classifications**: All MLS rules would be categorized as Mandatory, Recommended, Optional, or Informational. This system provided clarity regarding obligations and expectations for all participants.

- **Compensation Transparency**: New regulations require Agents to disclose compensation structures openly, ensuring Buyers and Sellers know precisely how much real estate professionals will earn. A critical point Sarah emphasized was that **no specific compensation amounts will be displayed in the MLS**. While this information would always be negotiable, it would not be included in Listings, helping to protect both Agent and Seller from potential conflicts of interest.

- **Enhanced Disclosure Requirements**: Under the Settlement, Agents were now mandated to disclose to both Sellers and Buyers that **Broker compensation is not set by law and is fully negotiable**. This disclosure must be included in conspicuous language as part of any Listing Agreement and Agent Agreement, empowering Clients with knowledge about their financial arrangements.

- **Written Agent Agreements**: New policies mandated that real estate Agents must enter into written agreements with Buyers before showing properties. This agreement outlines services to be provided and how compensation will be structured, providing Agents greater clarity and control over their transactions.

- **Ethical Standards and Cooperation**: The MLS now emphasizes cooperation, mandating that all real estate Agents share Listing information transparently. This collaborative spirit will help level the playing field and promote fair competition among real estate Agents.

- **Enhanced Dispute Resolution**: The new rules offered improved mechanisms for resolving conflicts between real estate Agents, particularly regarding compensation disputes, emphasizing fairness and maintaining trust.

Adapting to the Changes

As the seminar concluded, it was evident to Sarah and her colleagues that these changes would significantly impact how they conducted business. Many Agents had not received formal training in negotiation, compensation structures, or the legal implications of the Sherman Antitrust Act, but the evolving landscape required them to step up their game.

"Understanding these reforms is key to delivering exceptional service to our Client," Sarah emphasized. "We need to be well-informed and ready to explain these changes to Buyers and Sellers to assist them in navigating this new environment confidently."

The conversation shifted toward developing strategies for effectively communicating these ideas to Clients. "We want our Clients to know they are empowered with knowledge and options," Sarah reiterated. "Transparency breeds trust, and when they feel confident in the process, we all win."

Agent's Journey From Uncertainty to Empowerment

As the crisp autumn air swept through the neighborhood, Amy found herself standing outside a quaint open house, her heart racing with a blend of excitement and apprehension. The charming facade beckoned her closer, promising the perfect setting for her dreams of homeownership. But as she stepped inside, she quickly realized she was venturing into unfamiliar territory without a trusted guide.

It was a bustling Saturday, and the living room buzzed with chatter from other potential Buyers. Amy felt like a ship adrift at sea, surrounded by a flurry of information and eager voices discussing features, renovations, and potential offers. With no real estate professional accompanying her, she felt overwhelmed by the details swirling around her.

"Isn't this kitchen gorgeous?" a couple remarked, but Amy was too caught up in trying to remember the Listing price and the square footage to join in on the excitement. As she wandered from room to room, she tried to absorb the charm of the home, yet the pressure of deciding weighed heavily on her.

The Listing Agent, charming and persuasive, highlighted the home's virtues — its modern appliances, spacious backyard, and prime location — yet all the while, Amy felt a gnawing uncertainty in her gut. Without the support of an educated real estate professional, she was left to navigate this intricate labyrinth of real estate rules and unspoken protocols alone.

Everything felt daunting, especially the topic of compensation. Amy had heard whispers about how compensation structures worked, yet the details eluded her. The Listing Agent seemed to suggest that compensation would be vital in securing not just the property but a favorable position in negotiations if she decided to place an offer.

By the time she left the open house, Amy's mind swirled with information, confusion, and a sense of lost opportunity. She knew she needed an ally; someone who could alleviate her worries and help her make sense of the process. That night, she resolved to find a real estate professional who could navigate the complexities of the MLS with her, ensuring that she wouldn't face these crucial decisions alone again.

A few days later, Amy met Mike, a local real estate Agent known for his approachable demeanor and extensive knowledge of the market. As they sat down over coffee, she shared her open-house experience and the chaos she had encountered. Mike listened carefully, nodding as she spoke about the uncertainties she had faced about offers, compensation, and the lack of guidance.

"Let's break this down," Mike said, his voice steady and reassuring. "With the way the new MLS system works, you have the power to negotiate your terms and even determine how to compensate me as your Buyer's Agent. It's a different game now, and I'm here to empower you through every step."

As they explored the MLS platform together, Amy felt a wave of relief wash over her. With the Buyer's Agent Contract Agreement, they could clearly outline working terms and expectations. No longer shackled by the assumptions of the past, she could actively participate in the negotiation process, deciding how to structure the compensation based on her needs and preferences.

With Mike by her side, Amy began to view properties differently—not just as Listings, but as opportunities to engage and negotiate. Each show became an adventure, a chance to explore her desires and make informed decisions. Together, they navigated the market, discussing features and values in terms that resonated with her.

Eventually, Amy set sights on a lovely bungalow that met all her criteria. With confidence gained through Mike's guidance, she made a well-researched offer, clearly delineating the terms of compensation and envisioning her future in this new space.

When the call came to announce that Amy's offer was accepted, the joy felt surreal. This time, she wasn't just a passive participant; she was an empowered Buyer—educated, informed, and ready to embrace homeownership on her terms.

As Amy turned the key to her new home, an overwhelming sense of accomplishment washed over her. The path to homeownership had transformed from confusion to clarity, and she knew that it was the partnership with her Buyer's Agent, the transparency of the new MLS dynamics, and the ability to negotiate that had made all the difference.

In this evolving landscape, Amy's journey stood as a testament to the power of empowerment—of stepping into a new era where Buyers like her could navigate the home-buying process with confidence and control.

Updated Definition of MLS Participants:

The definition of an MLS participant has been amended to focus on cooperation:

- **New Definition**: Sellers are required to cooperate by sharing information on listed properties and making them available for showing to prospective Buyers and tenants, always in the best interest of their Sellers. Any references to offers of compensation have been removed.

- **A Commitment to Ethics and Fairness:** These changes represent a commitment to higher ethical standards, promoting a fair and transparent real estate marketplace. By adhering to these new policies, real estate professionals can enhance their practices, build trust with Clients, and navigate the evolving landscape effectively.

Update of Practice Changes and MLS information: Embracing Transformation in Real Estate

In light of the recent Settlement and subsequent policy changes mandated by the National Association's leadership, the real estate landscape is evolving to promote transparency, fairness, and professional integrity. Here's a summary of the critical changes that all real estate professionals and members of the industry need to remember:

- **Elimination of Compensation Offers in MLS Change**: Any requirement for Listing Broker or Seller to make offers of compensation to Buyer's Broker or other Agent representatives through the MLS has been eliminated and prohibited.

- **Definition of Cooperation Change**: The term "cooperation" is retained and clearly defined for MLS participation, emphasizing a collaborative spirit among Agents.

- **Prohibition of Compensation Officers and Compensation Fields**: MLS participants, subscribers, and Sellers are prohibited from posting offers of compensation on the MLS. All Broker compensation fields and related information must be removed from the MLS, ensuring that compensation details are not publicized.

- **Limitations on Non-MLS Platforms Change**: MLSs must not create, facilitate, or support any mechanisms outside of the MLS that allow offers of compensation to be made.

- **Data Usage Restriction Change**: The use of MLS data or feeds to establish or maintain platforms for offers of compensation from multiple Brokers must be prohibited, with violations leading to termination of access to MLS data.

- **Mandatory Compensation Disclosures Change**: Compensation disclosures to the Seller and the prospective Buyer Agent are now required, solidifying the foundation of transparency in transactions.

- **Written Agent Agreements Change**: Agents working with Buyers must enter into a written agreement with them before touring properties. This agreement must clearly outline compensation and services.

- **Updated Definition of MLS Participants**: The definition of an MLS participant has been amended to focus on cooperation. Participants are required to cooperate by sharing information on listed properties and making them available for showing prospective purchases and tenants, always in the best interest of their Clients. Any references to offers of compensation have been removed.

A Commitment to Ethics and Fairness

These changes represent a commitment to higher ethical standards, promoting a fair and transparent real estate marketplace. By adhering to these new policies, real estate professionals can enhance their practices, build trust with Clients, and navigate the evolving landscape effectively.

As we embrace these transformations, remember that *collaboration and communication are key to success. With a foundation built on clarity and integrity, the path forward in real estate is a promising on*e.

Key Points Summary:

- **Purpose:** The changes made aim to give Sellers more choice and flexibility in how their property is marketed while maintaining a system of openness within the MLS.
- **Delayed Marketing Exempt Listing:** This allows a property to be marketed through various channels (yard signs, websites, etc.) during a defined period *before* it's broadly advertised via IDX and syndication.
- **Access for MLS Participants:** Even during the delayed marketing period, the listing is fully available to other MLS participants.

- **Seller Disclosure:** A signed disclosure is required from the Seller, acknowledging they are waiving the benefits of immediate public marketing through IDX and syndication.
- **Active Listing:** Delayed marketing exempt listings are considered active listings, and showings are allowed (subject to the Seller's instructions and applicable law).
- **MLS Flexibility:** MLSs have some discretion in how they implement the policy.
- **No Prohibition of Showings:** MLSs cannot prohibit showings for delayed marketing-exempt listings.
- **VOW (Virtual Office Workplace) Data Feeds:** Delayed marketing exempt listings *must* be included in VOW data feeds.
- **Conversion Allowed:** Sellers can switch from an office-exclusive exempt listing to a delayed marketing exempt listing.
- **Advertising:** Sellers and their Brokers *can* advertise delayed marketing exempt listings on other websites, portals, social media, etc., during the delayed marketing period.
- **Data Feeds for Participants:** MLS participants can get a data feed of their listing information to display delayed marketing listings on other websites or portal.

Chapter 4

Mastering Negotiation Skills

To successfully represent Buyers, Sellers, and their respective Agents, mastering negotiation is essential. Confidence in your negotiation skills equips you to handle both Listing and Sales transactions with professionalism and strategy. This section lays the groundwork for negotiation fundamentals, followed by in-depth guides to both Seller and Buyer transactions.

Mastering Negotiation

As the crisp autumn leaves danced in the wind outside, Emily sat at her desk, preparing for a pivotal negotiation on behalf of her Client, Lisa, who was ready to sell her home. With the stakes high and everyone's future hanging in the balance, Emily understood that mastering negotiation was not merely about making offers and counteroffers—it was an art that demanded finesse, strategy, and empathy.

Setting Goals

Before initiating the negotiation process, Emily emphasized the importance of defining goals.

"Think of our goals as the compass guiding us through these discussions," she said, her voice calm and reassuring. "With clear objectives, we can navigate more confidently and make informed decisions."

Together, they mapped out Lisa's priorities:

Non-negotiable: Minimum sale price and move-out timeline.

Flexible: Closing costs, including appliances.

Bonus: Offers above asking price or waived contingencies.

Emily explained that by identifying what was essential versus negotiable, Lisa would feel more grounded when reviewing offers — reducing stress and making it easier to respond with confidence and clarity.

By the end of the conversation, Lisa felt empowered and prepared to enter the negotiation landscape.

The Role of Transparency in Negotiation

As they strategized, Emily recalled her recent training on the legal Settlement stemming from the Revolutionary Plaintiffs v. the National

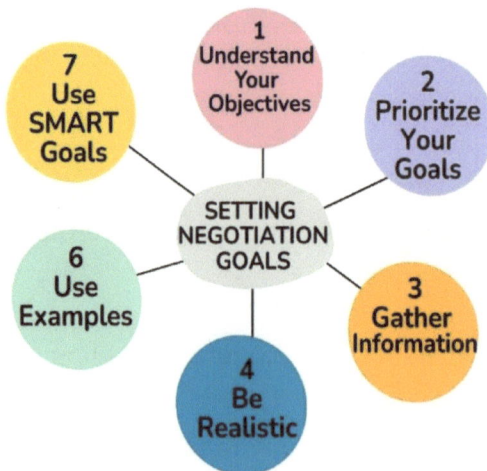

Association case, which placed significant emphasis on transparency within real estate practices. Understanding the vital role transparency played in negotiations, Emily knew that trust would be critical.

"Transparency means we communicate all terms, expectations, and potential outcomes clearly and openly," Emily explained to Lisa. "It's about ensuring we're both on the same page." Lisa nodded, appreciating Emily's commitment to keeping the lines of communication open. They agreed that being upfront about financial constraints, as well as any concerns or limitations, would prevent misunderstandings and foster a more collaborative negotiation atmosphere.

With their goals set and their commitment to transparency established, Emily felt ready to engage the Buyer's Agent. She took a deep breath, focusing on the essential task ahead.

Understanding Personalities in Negotiation

As Emily prepared for the upcoming negotiation, she knew that recognizing the Buyer's Agent's personality would be pivotal to her strategy. People process information in different ways, and adapting her communication style accordingly could significantly improve outcomes.

She began by considering the key personality types she might encounter:

• **The Analyzer**: Detail-oriented and cautious, this type thrived on data and facts. Emily knew that if the Buyer's Agent fell into this category, she would need to prepare thorough market reports and home appraisals to justify Lisa's asking price without pressuring the Agent.

• **The Driver**: Results-driven and decisive, a driver would necessitate a more concise approach focused on outcomes. Emily planned to highlight the property's value and efficiency of a swift transaction to resonate with a driver.

• **The Socializer**: Outgoing and relationship-focused, a socializer values connections and emotional appeal. Emily mused that if the Buyer's Agent connected with the home on a personal level, it might enhance her chances of a successful negotiation. "I'll share how Lisa's family enjoyed special moments in the house, which could establish an emotional bond," she noted.

• **The Relater**: Cooperative and empathetic, a relater sought trust and mutual benefits. For this personality type, she would emphasize transparency about any potential negotiation challenges, and building rapport through an honest exchange.

Emily reminded herself to observe subtle cues during the meeting—tone, pace, and choice of words—all of which would reveal the Agent's personality type and guide her strategy.

The Negotiation Begins

As she stepped into the meeting room, a wave of calm confidence settled over Emily. With clearly defined goals and a nuanced understanding of negotiation psychology, she felt prepared not just to represent Lisa—but to foster a negotiation built on trust and clarity.

The room buzzed with anticipation as she greeted the Buyer's Agent. This wasn't just about making a deal—it was about creating a win-win outcome, one grounded in professionalism and purpose. With every

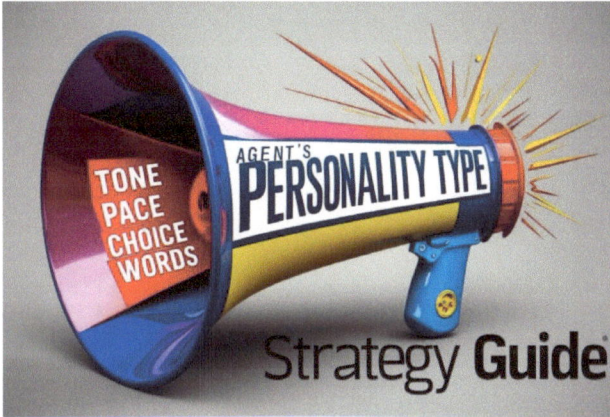

interaction, Emily stayed focused on the strategies she and Lisa had outlined, drawing on her training and instincts.

She knew that successful negotiation wasn't just transactional—it was transformational. And with each carefully chosen word and well-timed pause, Emily was ready to guide this deal toward a successful close for everyone involved.

Negotiation Strategies for: Real Estate Professionals, Buyers, and Sellers

As the sun dipped below the horizon, casting a golden glow over the suburban neighborhood, Emily sat at her desk, a cup of tea warming her hands as she prepared for an important negotiation meeting. She had always believed that negotiation was more than just swapping offers; it was a nuanced dance of understanding, strategizing, and trust-building.

Whether as a real estate professional, a Buyer seeking their dream home, or a Seller aiming to maximize their return, effective negotiation was essential to achieving goals. With a clear sense of purpose, Emily aimed to equip herself with actionable strategies that would help her Clients—and herself—navigate the complex negotiation landscape with confidence and success.

Step 1: Setting Clear Goals

Before the meeting began, Emily reminded herself of the first crucial step: setting clear goals. "My Clients' goals are truly my goals as well," she told herself. She recalled the earlier discussions she had with Lisa, her Client, about her priorities for selling her home. Lisa wanted not just to secure the highest possible price but also aimed for a swift sale to facilitate her move.

Emily had guided Lisa through some targeted questions to unearth her true intentions. Was Lisa focused primarily on a quick sale, or did maximizing her return on the home take precedence? They broke these goals into specific categories: primary and secondary objectives.

For Lisa, the primary goals involved establishing a non-negotiable minimum acceptable price. Meanwhile, secondary goals included her preferred closing date and terms she was willing to offer, such as making repairs or providing warranties.

When it came to Buyers, Emily encouraged them to clarify their ideal purchase price, acceptable contingencies, and potential concessions they might seek, like assistance with closing costs. As she reviewed her notes, Emily ranked these goals by importance, recognizing that knowing what mattered most would enable her to remain firm where necessary and flexible where it counted.

Step 2: Structuring Negotiation Meetings

As Emily reviewed her agenda, she prepared to structure the negotiation meeting thoughtfully. A well-organized discussion would create a secure environment that minimizes misunderstandings.

"Preparation is key," she reminded herself, conducting thorough research on the market and comparable properties. Anticipating objections ahead of time allowed her to craft informed responses— an essential strategy for effective negotiations.

When the moment arrived, Emily began the meeting with an icebreaker, sharing a lighthearted story about her weekend. This rapport-building moment helped break the tension and set a positive tone for the discussion. She then presented the key points, carefully limiting her initial presentation to three main concepts. Overloading the other party with information could easily lead to disengagement or confusion.

"Encouraging open dialogue is essential," she thought, guiding the conversation by asking open-ended questions. "What's most important to you in this transaction?" she inquired, allowing her Clients to express their needs and priorities.

As the conversation unfolded, Emily recapped their discussion and laid out the agreed-upon next steps. This structure fostered trust and kept the focus on solutions rather than obstacles, helping everyone feel confident about the path forward.

Step 3: How to Address Common Objections

During the negotiation, Emily was prepared for objections— viewing them not as roadblocks but as opportunities to build a better understanding. When a Seller expressed concerns about pricing—I think the price is too high"—Emily acknowledged their apprehension. "I understand pricing is critical, especially in today's market," she replied, validating their feelings before guiding the conversation toward a solution.

"Let's look at comparable sales in the area to ensure the price aligns with market value," Emily suggested, presenting data that supported her rationale. This approach demonstrated her willingness to collaborate, creating an atmosphere of trust.

Next, when addressing questions about compensation, Emily reassured her Clients. "It's a valid question, especially with the recent changes in the market," she acknowledged. "Offering compensation can attract qualified Buyers, leading to a faster sale at the price you desire."

When the timing of decisions became an issue, she listened carefully, responding with empathy. "It's important to feel confident about your decision. What additional information can I provide to help you move forward?" This demonstrated her commitment to supporting their journey, reinforcing trust further.

Throughout the negotiation, Emily took note of nonverbal cues— body language, tone, and facial expressions—ensuring she remained attuned to unspoken concerns. She valued the emotional landscape of the negotiation, recognizing that validating emotions was crucial during this intense process. "I can see why you'd feel frustrated about the timing," she would say, before exploring options that could work for everyone involved.

Listening Pitfalls to Avoid

Emily was keenly aware of common listening pitfalls that could derail negotiations. She steered clear of jumping to conclusions, remaining open to her Clients' perspectives without making assumptions. Interruptions could diminish the value of their input, and she consciously avoided interjecting.

While she maintained a focused agenda, Emily also prioritized the concerns voiced during discussions, understanding that addressing the emotional landscape could stall progress if neglected. Instead of listening to identify weaknesses in arguments, she approached negotiations with a mindset aimed at understanding the challenges, working to build constructive bridges.

The Power of Effective Negotiation

As the meeting progressed and Emily navigated the intricate web of negotiation, she felt a gratifying sense of fulfillment. The strategies she had prepared, the rapport she had built, and the commitment to transparency all contributed to a seamless, goal-aligned process.

Each successful exchange didn't just move the deal forward—it strengthened her relationships. Through clear, effective negotiation,

Emily empowered her Clients to feel confident in their decisions. These were more than transactions; they were moments of trust, collaboration, and progress.

The Power of Flexibility in Negotiations

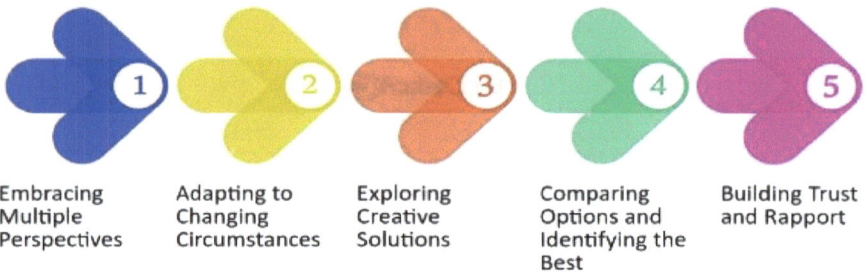

1	2	3	4	5
Embracing Multiple Perspectives	Adapting to Changing Circumstances	Exploring Creative Solutions	Comparing Options and Identifying the Best	Building Trust and Rapport

In the world of real estate, the true power of negotiation lies in its ability to create connections—not just close deals. With every agreement she facilitated, Emily found herself growing—not only as a professional but as a trusted guide in her Clients' journey toward their dreams.

Step 4: How to Address Common Objections

As Emily prepared for her next meeting, she recalled a fundamental principle of negotiation: objections are not roadblocks—they are opportunities. In her experience as a real estate professional, every objection raised during negotiation was a chance to uncover concerns and build trust. She reminded herself that by addressing objections skillfully, she could demonstrate her willingness to collaborate and find solutions that worked for everyone involved.

Price Concerns

Another common objection centered on Buyer or Seller Agent's compensation, particularly in light of recent industry changes. Clients might ask:
"Who should pay the Buyer's Agent compensation?"

Emily acknowledged the question's importance:

"That's a valid concern, especially with the shifts we've seen in the industry."

Then she confidently reframed the objection:

"Offering competitive compensation can help attract qualified Buyers, which ultimately leads to a quicker sale—often at your target price."

By emphasizing the *strategic value* of compensation, Emily not only addressed the objection but also educated her Clients—highlighting how thoughtful choices in negotiation impact results.

Agent Compensation Concerns

Another common objection centered on Seller's Agent compensation, particularly in light of recent industry changes. Clients might ask: "Who should pay the Buyer's Agent compensation?"

Emily acknowledged the question's importance:

"That's a valid concern, especially with the shifts we've seen in the industry."

Then she confidently reframed the objection:

"Offering competitive compensation can help attract qualified Buyer's, which ultimately leads to a quicker sale—often at your target price."

By emphasizing the *strategic value* of compensation, Emily not only addressed the objection but also educated her Clients, highlighting how thoughtful choices in negotiation impact results.

Timing Issues

Seasoned negotiators often face Sellers experiencing timing issues—especially decision fatigue during critical moments of a sale. Emily had heard it many times: "I'm not ready to make a decision yet." Recognizing the significance of this hesitation, she would gently acknowledge, "It's important to feel confident about your decision." This validation resonated, affirming that the Seller's feelings were not just heard but respected.

To assist Clients in moving forward, she would then offer a solution: "What additional information can I provide to help you move forward?" By inviting dialogue and expressing a genuine interest in her Client's comfort level, Emily could help alleviate any anxiety and foster a productive conversation.

Key Strategies for Addressing Objections

As Emily engaged in these discussions, she kept several important strategies in mind:

• **Validate Concerns Before Solutions**: Always validating concerns allowed Clients to feel acknowledged. This reassurance was key to fostering trust and helped set a positive tone for problem-solving.

• **Use Open-Ended Questions**: Asking open-ended questions was another tool Emily wielded with intention. Inquiring, "Can you tell me more about why that's important to you?" deepened conversations and revealed specific motivations that could further inform negotiations.

• **Pause before Responding**: Emily practiced the art of pausing before responding. She knew that a moment of silence signaled her consideration of the Seller's words, helping prevent interruptions while allowing time to formulate a thoughtful response.

• **Pay Attention to Nonverbal Cues**: Being vigilant about body language, tone, and facial expressions was essential. These nonverbal signals often reveal unspoken concerns or emotions that might not be conveyed through words.

• **Acknowledge Emotions with Empathy**: Emily understood the weight of emotions in negotiations. Acknowledging feelings helped her demonstrate empathy. "I can see why you'd feel frustrated about the timing, let's explore some options that could work for you," became a common phrase. It reinforced her commitment to finding solutions that worked for both parties.

Listening Pitfalls to Avoid

Emily remained mindful of several common listening pitfalls that could jeopardize the negotiation process. She made a conscious effort to avoid jumping to conclusions, reminding herself to remain open to her Clients' perspectives. Equally important, she resisted the urge to interrupt—knowing that doing so could leave any Client feeling dismissed or undervalued.

While staying focused on their established goals was essential, Emily also understood that disregarding Client concerns could derail negotiations entirely. To maintain balance, she committed to listening with intent—not to find flaws or counter arguments, but to genuinely understand challenges and build bridges toward collaborative solutions.

With these strategies firmly in place, Emily approached each conversation with a sense of clarity and confidence. These discussions weren't merely about contracts and pricing; they were about connection, trust, and crafting thoughtful solutions that led to success for everyone involved.

The Power of Listening in Negotiation

As Emily prepared for the upcoming negotiation session, she settled into her chair and closed her eyes for a moment, envisioning the room filled with potential. Today was not just about transactions; it was about understanding the nuances of people, their concerns, and the relationships that would shape the future. With a deep breath, she reminded herself of the vital role that listening would play in today's discussion.

Negotiation was often equated with what one said—offers thrown across the table, counter offers, and strategic claims. But Emily knew better; she understood that true negotiation power lay in the art of listening. In real estate, emotions ran high, finances were on the line, and long-term commitments loomed. The ability to listen could mean the difference between a fruitful agreement or a missed opportunity.

Why Listening Matters in Negotiation

As she reflected on past negotiations, Emily recalled the countless times that active listening had helped her build trust with Clients. When they felt heard, it paved the way for deeper relationships and meaningful dialogue. During one particularly challenging negotiation, she listened intently as the Sellers expressed their concerns about timing due to a personal relocation. By acknowledging their urgency, she was able to reassure them that their needs would be a priority in the negotiation. This small act of empathy not only gained their trust but also facilitated a collaborative atmosphere where honest discussions thrived.

Emily understood that beneath the surface of initial statements often lay hidden priorities. A seemingly straightforward Seller might be driven by urgent motivations rooted in personal circumstances. As she entered each negotiation, Emily stayed vigilant, recognizing that every Client and Agent left subtle clues about their true concerns.

Through attentive listening, she had often uncovered these underlying motivations: a Seller eager to close quickly due to a job relocation, or a Buyer seeking specific concessions to ease financial strain. Identifying these deeper needs allowed Emily to craft solutions that were not only strategic but also empathetic moving beyond the transaction to foster genuine collaboration.

Moreover, Emily realized that her attentiveness fostered cooperation. When she actively listened, her Client's reciprocated, creating a dynamic where both parties were more inclined to work together. This collaborative atmosphere diminished defensiveness and built a foundation for mutual problem-solving, turning potential conflicts into opportunities for innovation and compromise.

Active Listening Techniques

To harness the power of listening effectively, Emily employed several active listening techniques.

- **Stay Present**: Emily was mindful of distractions. She avoided checking her phone or allowing her mind to wander to her next response while her Clients were speaking. Instead, she practiced nonverbal engagement, nodding along and maintaining eye contact, demonstrating her undivided attention.

- **Reflect and Clarify**: Emily found that repeating or paraphrasing key points was instrumental in ensuring understanding. "If I understand correctly," she would begin, "your priority is a quick closing date. Is that right?" This approach not only confirmed her understanding but also made her Client's feel valued, reinforcing the rapport they had built.

- **Ask Open-Ended Questions**: Another technique she employed was to pose open-ended questions that encouraged her Client's to elaborate on their thoughts. "Can you tell me more about what's most important to you in this transaction?" Emily would ask, providing Client's with the space to voice their anxieties and desires.

As Emily entered the negotiation meeting, she felt equipped. The knowledge that listening was more than a skill, but a strategy would guide her success. In her heart, she knew that the ability to truly hear and understand the needs of both Sellers and Buyers would empower her to negotiate with confidence and cultivate lasting relationships— transforming negotiations from mere business transactions into collaborative journeys toward shared success, ultimately leading to a successful negotiation.

Case Study 1: Selling a Family Home
Scenario: Submitting Counteroffer and Closing Costs

Jessica, a Seller, has listed her charming three-bedroom home for $320,000. After receiving an offer from Tom, a first-time Buyer who is eager to make this house his home, they enter into negotiations. However, Tom's offer comes in at $300,000, and he is also requesting the Seller to cover his closing costs due to budget constraints.

How It Played Out

Jessica, feeling slightly disappointed by Tom's initial offer, knew she could not simply reject it. Instead, she sought the assistance of her Agent, Michelle, to facilitate a constructive dialogue.

Michelle advised Jessica to counteroffer at $315,000 while willing to cover half of Tom's closing costs. The aim was to acknowledge Tom's position while ensuring Jessica still felt satisfied with the sale price. They presented their counteroffer, emphasizing how much Jessica valued the home and wanted to make a fair deal.

Tom's Buyer's Agent, Lisa, received the counteroffer and conveyed Jessica's willingness to compromise, which opened the door for further negotiations. Tom, appreciating Jessica's flexibility, was encouraged to increase his offer to $310,000 and agreed to accept the closing cost assistance as part of the deal.

Through continuous communication, both parties navigated the negotiation successfully, ultimately agreeing on a sale price of $312,500, with Jessica covering the closing costs up to a specified amount. Both sides felt satisfied with the arrangement, allowing Tom to purchase his dream home while respecting Jessica's needs.

Key Strategy: Collaborative Negotiation

The key strategy that made this negotiation successful was collaborative negotiation. By focusing on shared interests—such as Jessica's need to sell the home at a fair price and Tom's need for financial assistance—both parties could constructively compromise while fostering a relationship built on trust and respect.

Practice Suggestion for Buyer's Agent and Seller's Agent

To enhance negotiation skills and foster rapport-building, consider the following practice activity:

Role-Playing Negotiation Scenarios

• **Activity**: Set up role-playing exercises where participants take turns acting as the Seller, the Buyer, and their respective Agents. Create varied scenarios where negotiation points differ, such as price, closing costs, repair requests, or timelines.

• **Engagement**: During the role-playing session, encourage Agents to engage with each other by asking questions about priorities and concerns. This builds rapport and hones their ability to communicate effectively under pressure.

• **Presenting Key Points**: Part of this exercise includes refining the ability to communicate value clearly and concisely. Each participant should present their position, focusing on two or three key selling points or values they want to communicate.

- **Feedback**: After each role-play, participants can provide constructive feedback on clarity, empathy, and negotiation tactics used.

Recap on "How it played out"

In the negotiation process between Jessica and Tom, the key negotiation skills that helped them successfully navigate the situation included:

1. **Empathy and Understanding**: Both parties demonstrated a genuine willingness to understand each other's situations, fostering a collaborative atmosphere.

2. **Flexibility**: Jessica's willingness to adjust her price and cover partial closing costs allowed for a compromise that satisfied both parties.

3. **Effective Communication**: Michelle, as the Seller's Agent, was instrumental in articulating the value of the home and Jessica's priorities, ensuring the Buyer Tom understood the rationale behind the counteroffer.

4. **Trust Building**: A spirit of cooperation enabled both Seller Jessica and Buyer Tom to trust one another, leading to a positive negotiation outcome.

Key Strategy Description

The success of this negotiation ultimately stemmed from a collaborative approach, where both the Buyers and Sellers were invested in a solution that met their needs. This strategy emphasized the importance of communication, empathy, and a willingness to find common ground. By understanding and addressing the concerns of each party, they not only secured a deal but also laid the groundwork for a positive experience that may lead to referrals and future business opportunities.

Case Study 2: Negotiating Inspection Repairs

Scenario: First-time Home Buyer's Post-Inspection Concerns

Sarah and Daniel, first-time home Buyer's, were thrilled when their offer was accepted on a charming bungalow. But their excitement dimmed slightly after the home inspection revealed a few issues—including minor roof repairs and a faulty furnace. While the appraisal came back positive, the couple grew concerned about how the repairs might affect their finances.

How It Played Out

Turning to their Buyer's Agent, Mike, for guidance, Sarah and Daniel sought a way forward. Mike encouraged them to approach the situation collaboratively rather than confrontationally. He recommended they create a list of necessary repairs, complete with estimated costs, to present a clear and reasonable request.

When the couple shared their concerns with the Seller, Laura, through her Seller's Agent, Emily, they began the conversation on a positive note. They expressed appreciation for the home's features and excitement about the purchase—while also being transparent about their concerns.

"I understand how stressful it can be to receive news of repairs," Emily said, validating their concerns while carefully reviewing the request with Laura.

Recognizing the fairness of the approach and appreciating the respectful tone, Laura agreed to repair the furnace and offered a $1,500 credit toward closing costs to offset the roof repairs.

The outcome was a win-win: Sarah and Daniel secured their dream home with peace of mind, and Laura met her sales objectives. Both sides felt respected and empowered proof that effective negotiation is rooted in empathy, clarity, and collaboration.

Key Strategy: Empathy-Driven Negotiation

The key strategy was empathy-driven negotiation. By acknowledging and validating the emotional response to unexpected inspection issues, all parties found common ground that led to satisfactory solutions.

Practice Suggestion

Team Review Sessions

• Gather in a group to discuss past negotiations, focusing on situations that involved inspection-related concerns.

• Role-play the approach for each party (Buyer, Sellers, Agents) utilizing empathy to navigate concerns about repairs.

• Encourage feedback on how well each party handled emotional responses and communicated effectively.

Case Study 3: Competing Offers in a Hot Market

Scenario: A Competitive Bidding War for Popular Property

Kat recently found her dream home, which generated multiple offers in a competitive market. She made a solid offer, but to win the bidding war, her Buyer's Agent, James, needed to strategize effectively while maintaining Kat's budget.

How It Played Out

Buyer's Agent James quickly identified his Client Kat's non-negotiable maximum price, while also highlighting her strongest features as a Buyer: pre-approval for financing and a flexible closing date. To enhance the offer, James recommended adding a personal touch—a heartfelt letter from Kat expressing why she loved the home and how it would become a cherished space for her family.

(Note from the author: In more than 50% of transactions, I write a personal letter to the Seller on behalf of my Clients—a strategy that has consistently proven effective.)

When submitting the revised offer, Buyer Kat agreed to slightly increase her offer price and focused on showcasing elements that might resonate with the Sellers, who were downsizing and likely had an emotional attachment to the home. Buyer's Agent James emphasized Kat's financial readiness and her genuine emotional connection to the property.

In the end, it was this thoughtful combination—financial viability, flexibility, and a heartfelt connection—that helped Kat stand out in a competitive market. The Seller's accepted her offer, feeling confident that their beloved home would be well cared for and deeply appreciated.

Key Strategy: Personalization in Negotiation

The key strategy that emerged was personalization in negotiation. By weaving emotional narratives into their strategy, they increased the appeal of the Buyer Kat's offer, setting it apart from the competition.

Practice Suggestion

Personal Story Mapping

- Organize a workshop where Seller's and Buyer's create personal narratives that highlight their values and motivations related to home ownership.

- Participants can practice how to present these stories effectively during negotiations to connect with Sellers emotionally.

- Role-play sessions can be introduced to simulate presenting personalized offers alongside financial ones.

Case Study 4: Creative Financing Solutions

Scenario: A Buyer's Challenge with Down Payment Savings

Brian and Julia were eager to purchase their first home, but with their down payment funds falling short in a competitive market, they were feeling discouraged. They sought the assistance of Jessica, their Buyer's Agent, to develop a creative solution.

How It Played Out

Jessica knew that to help her Client's, Brian and Julia, compete in a competitive market without exceeding their budget, they needed a smart, strategic approach. During their meeting, they explored options such as down payment assistance programs and requesting seller contributions toward closing costs.

Buyer's Agent Jessica recommended structuring the offer to include a request for the Seller to cover part of the closing costs. This would allow Brian and Julia to redirect more of their available funds toward a stronger down payment—making their offer more attractive while keeping their finances intact.

With a confident and well-crafted offer that emphasized their financial readiness and commitment to homeownership, they submitted their proposal.

The Seller—motivated by the opportunity for a quicker sale and reassured by Jessica's professionalism—agreed to the closing cost assistance. Thanks to thoughtful planning and negotiation, First Time

Buyer's Brian and Julia secured their dream home without compromising their financial stability.

Key Strategy: Creative Problem-Solving

The strategy that led to success was creative problem-solving. By seeking innovative financing solutions, they overcame barriers that initially seemed insurmountable.

Practice Suggestion Brainstorming Solutions Workshop

- Conduct a workshop where participants can explore various financial strategies, availability of assistance programs, and creative solutions to home-buying limitations.

- Encourage group brainstorming sessions to generate unique approaches to address financial or negotiation challenges they may face.

- Role-play scenarios where participants practice creatively presenting their solutions to Sellers and other Agents.

Case Study 5: Handling Emotionally Charged Negotiations

Scenario: Divorcing Couple Selling Their Shared Home

Seller's Mark and Lisa needed to sell their shared home following their recent divorce. Both were emotionally charged during the process, complicating the negotiation landscape as they navigated their priorities.

How It Played Out

Recognizing the sensitivity of the situation, their Seller's Agent, Sarah, approached the negotiation with a strong emphasis on emotional intelligence. Sarah created a calm, respectful environment that encouraged both Seller's, Mark and Lisa, to express their concerns—without escalating tensions.

Sarah opened the meeting by giving each party space to share their feelings about the home and the sale. Through active listening, she validated their emotions and set a collaborative tone:

"I understand this is a difficult transition for both of you. We must get through this together—let's focus on creating a win-win situation."

Once both individuals felt heard, Sarah shifted the conversation toward their individual goals. Seller Mark prioritized maximizing the sale price, while Seller Lisa's focus was on a quick sale to support her upcoming move. By reframing the discussion around shared outcomes, Sarah proposed strategies that could serve both interests—such as agreeing on a minimum sale price with flexible closing terms.

After a series of respectful, goal-oriented negotiations, Sarah successfully mediated an agreement that honored the priorities of both Client's. The home sold under mutually acceptable terms, and the transaction helped resolve their differences amicably.

Key Strategy: Emotional Intelligence in Negotiation

The central strategy used during negotiations was emotional intelligence. By prioritizing empathy and understanding, Seller's Agent Sarah managed to facilitate a productive and respectful negotiation atmosphere.

Practice Suggestion: Emotional Awareness Training

- Host sessions focused on developing emotional intelligence skills, including active listening, empathy, and conflict resolution strategies.

- Use role-playing activities that simulate emotionally charged negotiations to help participants practice emotional regulation and effective communication.

- Encourage team discussions on how to apply emotional intelligence in their negotiations to cultivate a supportive and collaborative negotiating culture.

Case Study 6: Negotiating a Delay in Closing Scenario:
Buyers Encountering Financing Delays

Buyer's Paul and Megan were excited to purchase their first home after months of searching. With their offer accepted, they eagerly anticipated the closing day. However, as the closing date approached, their lender notified them of unexpected delays in the financing approval due to procedural issues. Faced with the possibility of postponing the closing indefinitely, they reached out to their Buyer's Agent, Sarah, for guidance.

How It Played Out

Upon learning about the financing delays, Buyer's Agent Sarah immediately arranged a meeting with the Seller's Agent, Tom. During the meeting, Sarah communicated the situation transparently, ensuring Tom understood the challenges her Clients were facing. "I want to be upfront," she said sincerely. "We're actively working to resolve this delay, but it's important to discuss potential options."

Understanding the potential frustration, Sarah suggested a creative compromise: "What if we propose extending the closing date by two weeks? In the meantime, we could offer to rent the home back to the Seller for that period at a nominal fee, ensuring they still have access to the property while waiting for us to finalize our financing."

Tom appreciated Sarah's proactive approach and agreed to discuss the proposition with his Seller's. After consulting with them, he returned with a counterproposal allowing for the delayed closing and noted that the Sellers would agree to the rental back terms. This agreement eased the pressure on both sides, preserving the deal while keeping everyone's interests intact.

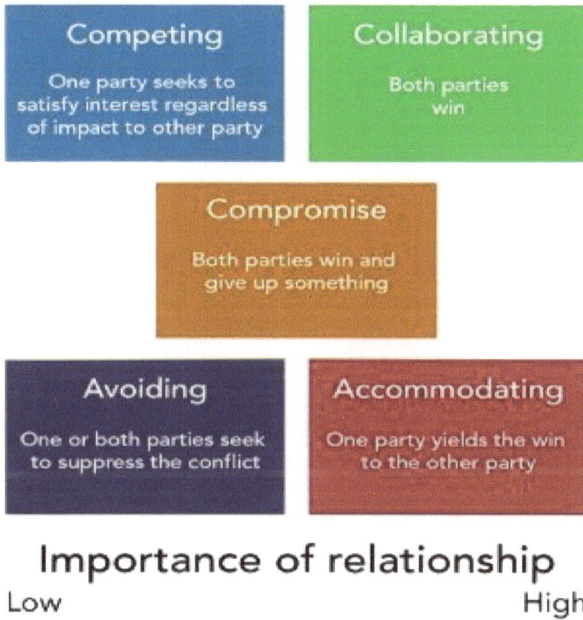

Key Strategy: Transparency and Collaboration

The key strategy utilized in this scenario was transparency and collaboration. By openly discussing the challenges and proposing creative solutions, Sarah fostered a sense of trust that ultimately helped keep the deal intact.

Practice Suggestion Collaboration Brainstorming Sessions

- Facilitate sessions where Agents can practice transparency in challenging negotiations, sharing their experiences and strategies for overcoming difficulties.

- Role-play potential scenarios where delays or issues arise and collaborate on how to effectively communicate both challenges and solutions.

- Emphasize the importance of proposing creative compromises that benefit all parties involved.

Case Study 7: Navigating Multiple Offers with Finesse
Scenario: Seller Receiving Multiple Offers

Seller Lisa had just listed her home and was excited to receive multiple offers within a week. With offers ranging from $450,000 to $475,000, she sought the expertise of her Seller's Agent, Emily, to ensure she made an informed decision that aligned with her goals.

How It Played Out

Emily quickly recognized the opportunity that multiple offers presented and initiated a strategy session with Seller Lisa. They first reviewed each offer in detail, examining not just the price but also the terms, contingencies, and closing timelines. The Seller, Lisa's priority, was to secure the best price, but she also wanted a quick closing to facilitate her relocation.

Understanding the competitive advantage they held, Emily recommended issuing a "highest and best" request to all potential Buyers, inviting them to resubmit their offers with their best terms. "This will let us see who is truly serious about purchasing your home," Emily explained, ensuring Lisa felt confident about the process.

The next day, Seller's Agent Emily sent out the request, reinforcing the value of Lisa's home and the ongoing interest. As the new offers came pouring in—this time with more favorable terms—Emily and Lisa summarized each proposal and focused on the ones that matched Lisa's goals.

Ultimately, they received an offer of $485,000 from a Buyer wanting to waive contingencies, which gave Lisa the peace of mind she needed. They accepted this offer and proceeded to a successful closing within 30 days.

Key Strategy: Utilizing Competitive Leveraging

The key strategy employed here was utilizing competitive leveraging. By creating an environment that encouraged Buyers to present their highest offers, Emily empowered Lisa to maximize her return while securing favorable terms.

Practice Suggestion Competitive Offer Workshops

- Conduct workshops where Agents can learn to leverage multiple offers effectively. Role-play scenarios where Agents present multiple offers to Clients and practice communicating value.

- Encourage Agents to share their own past experiences of navigating competitive offers, focusing on strategies that led to successful outcomes.

- Discuss methods to build rapport with Agents during competitive offer situations to create a positive atmosphere throughout the negotiation.

The Impact of Settlement Practices on Home Sellers

As Lisa sat down with Emily, her trusted real estate Agent, she considered the recent changes in the real estate landscape stemming from the Settlement associated with the Revolutionary Plaintiffs case. The shift in practices brought a wave of additional choices and transparency, empowering Sellers like herself as they prepared to navigate the complex world of home sales.

Empowered Choices and Transparency

"First and foremost, it's important to understand that these new practices empower you as a consumer, giving you more choices and transparency when selling your home," Emily began, laying out the benefits of the Settlement.

Lisa listened intently as Emily explained the importance of the compensation structure. "You still have the choice of offering compensation to Buyer Agents," she noted. "This can be a strategic way of marketing your home and making your Listing more appealing to potential Buyers."

Clear Communication and Approval

Emily emphasized the importance of adhering to the updated disclosure requirements regarding compensation arrangements.

"As your Agent, I am required to disclose any payments or offers made to the Buyer's Agent and obtain your approval in advance," she explained to Lisa. "This disclosure must be in writing and include the specific amount or rate. It adds an extra layer of protection and builds confidence for you as the Seller."

Lisa nodded, appreciating the clarity.

"So, we'll know the details of what compensation looks like before making any agreements?"

"100% correct," Emily replied with a reassuring smile. "If you choose to offer compensation to a Buyer's Agent, there are new rules around how that's communicated. For example, Seller's Agent can no longer include compensation details in the MLS—but that doesn't limit your broader marketing options."

Exploring Off-MLS Marketing Strategies

Emily continued, "Your Listing can still be marketed on off-MLS platforms like social media, flyers, and various real estate websites. This opens up a wider audience for your home, leveraging modern marketing to enhance visibility."

"That's good to know," Lisa responded, feeling reassured about her options. "And what about Buyer concessions?"

"You can still offer concessions for Buyer closing costs," Emily explained. "This flexibility is crucial in making your property more attractive to Buyer's, particularly in competitive markets."

Negotiable Agent Compensation

As their conversation continued, Emily reminded Lisa,

"Compensation for your Agent is entirely negotiable and is not dictated by law. If your Agent is a real estate professional, they are required to adhere to the Real Estate Code of Ethics, which mandates clear and transparent discussions regarding compensation."

Lisa nodded thoughtfully.

"It's important for me to feel comfortable and informed about these details."

Emily smiled, offering reassurance.

"When choosing an Agent, always ask about compensation and understand the services you'll receive in return. Your peace of mind is crucial in this process."

With newfound clarity and understanding, Lisa felt empowered by the Settlement practices designed to safeguard her interests as the Seller. The emphasis on greater transparency and flexibility reinforced the importance of making informed decisions in real estate transactions.

As she and Emily prepared to move forward, Lisa was grateful for the heightened awareness around compensation and the range of options available to her. Confident in her choices, she felt prepared to begin selling her home—knowing that she could navigate the process with transparency, trust, and the support she needed.

Summary

The Skills of Negotiation in Real Estate and Beyond

Negotiation is a vital skill that transcends industries, serving as a cornerstone for successful interactions and transactions. While the fundamental principles of negotiation remain consistent across various fields—whether in business, law, finance, or personal relationships—its application is especially pronounced in the real estate industry. Here, effective negotiation can mean the difference between a missed opportunity and a successful deal.

Key Skills of Negotiation

- **Active Listening**: Successful negotiation begins with the ability to listen actively. This entails understanding not only what the other party is saying but also recognizing underlying emotions and priorities. In real estate, this skill helps Agents identify Clients' needs, build trust, and foster productive discussions.

- **Clear Communication**: Articulating goals, offers, and concerns is essential in any negotiation. Real estate professionals must convey their Clients' interests and positions effectively, ensuring that all parties understand the terms of the deal. Clear communication mitigates misunderstandings and facilitates smoother transactions.

- **Empathy and Emotional Intelligence**: The ability to empathize with others fosters a collaborative atmosphere in negotiations. Agents who demonstrate an understanding of their Clients' feelings and concerns can better navigate the emotional aspects of selling or buying a home. Emotional intelligence enables negotiators to respond thoughtfully to objections and challenges.

- **Problem-Solving**: Negotiation often involves overcoming obstacles and finding mutually beneficial solutions. Flexibility in adapting strategies and proposing creative compromises is a valuable skill in real estate, particularly when faced with low appraisals, financing issues, or Buyer-Seller conflicts.

- **Strategic Planning and Preparation**: Successful negotiators conduct thorough research and establish clear goals before entering into discussions. In real estate, this includes understanding market conditions, property values, and the Buyer's preferences. Adequate preparation empowers Agents to negotiate from a position of strength and confidence.

- **Building Rapport and Relationships**: Establishing a positive rapport with Clients and opposing parties enhances cooperation and trust. In real estate, strong relationships can lead to referrals, repeat business, and successful negotiations that benefit all involved.

- **Persuasion and Influence**: The ability to persuade others to consider a particular viewpoint or solution is crucial in negotiation. Agents must effectively advocate for their Clients while also understanding the motivations and objections of the other party.

Application across Industries

While the listed skills are essential in real estate, they are equally relevant across various sectors, including:

- **Business**: In corporate environments, negotiation skills are critical for securing contracts, partnerships, and mergers.

- **Law**: Lawyers must negotiate settlements, and plea deals while advocating for their Clients' best interests.

- **Finance**: Negotiators in finance engage in discussions surrounding investment terms, loan agreements, and risk assessments.

- **Healthcare**: Negotiations in healthcare involve discussions regarding treatment costs, insurance reimbursements, and provider contracts.

In summary, negotiation skills are universally applicable yet particularly vital in the real estate industry. From understanding Client goals to navigating emotional dynamics, effective negotiation promotes favorable outcomes and fosters enduring relationships, leading to satisfaction for all parties involved. By mastering these skills, real estate professionals can navigate the complexities of transactions with confidence, ultimately driving success and growth in their careers.

The *Revolutionary Plaintiffs* v. the National Association Settlement has ushered in significant changes in the real estate industry, designed to enhance fairness and transparency for consumers. Here's a concise breakdown of the benefits resulting from the Settlement:

Clear Compensation Information:

- **Benefit:** Both Buyer and Seller Client's will now gain clarity on how much real estate professionals earn and how compensation is determined and split.

- **Client Impact:** No more confusion about financial allocations; Clients will see the costs and compensation involved in their transactions.

Empowered New Consumer:

- **Benefit**: With enhanced access to information, consumers can select services that fit their needs and budget.

- **Client Impact**: Negotiating better deals becomes possible, allowing Clients to avoid hidden costs and feel more in control of their transactions.

Fair Competition among Agents:

- **Benefit**: Outdated practices that limit consumer choices have been eliminated, enabling more Agents to compete for business.

- **Client Impact**: Consumers now have access to a broader range of services and the freedom to choose the best professional Agent for their needs without restrictions.

Potentially Lower Fees for Consumers:

- **Benefit**: Increased competition and transparency could lead to reduced compensation fees.

- **Client Impact**: Buying or selling a home may become more affordable, particularly for first-time Homebuyers.

Better Access to Property Information:

- **Benefit**: Clients can access more detailed property Listings directly from sources.

- **Client Impact**: Better-informed Clients can make smarter decisions about the properties they are interested in.

Support for New Business Models for Consumers:

- **Benefit**: Changes encourage innovative real estate services, including discount Brokers and flat-fee services.

- **Client Impact**: More options empower Clients to select the services that suit their preferences best.

Higher Standards for Real Estate Professionals:

- **Benefit**: Stricter guidelines ensure that Agents uphold transparency and represent Clients effectively.

- **Client Impact**: Clients can work with professionals committed to ethical standards, leading to smoother and more trustworthy experiences.

Ongoing Oversight and Improvements:

- **Benefit**: Continuous monitoring will ensure that the changes are effective and beneficial.

- **Client Impact**: Clients can feel confident in the evolving industry landscape, benefiting from ongoing improvements and enhanced practices.

Overall, the changes initiated by the Settlement hold the potential to reshape the real estate landscape, ensuring more transparency, fairness, and improved experiences for all participants.

Conclusion

As the real estate industry continued to evolve, the Settlement was entered into law on November 26, 2024. Ongoing efforts to monitor and refine these changes remain a top priority for many professionals in the field. Our commitment to staying updated and advocating for the best interests of our Clients ensures that your real estate experience will be not only easier but also more transparent and fairer. Rest assured, we have your back every step of the way, empowering you to navigate your buying and selling journey with confidence and support. Together, we can capitalize on the empowered consumer landscape created by these pivotal changes, leading to successful and fulfilling real estate transactions.

Chapter 5

Real estate Sellers should be well informed about the transaction process and the responsibilities undertaken by their Agents. Education empowers Sellers to make confident, informed decisions throughout the sales journey.

Sellers and Listing Agents

As Buyers and Sellers navigate the evolving world of real estate, they must understand the significant changes introduced by the **Revolutionary Plaintiffs case** and the resulting **Settlement**. These legal shifts have reshaped key aspects of the real estate industry, especially in how properties are marketed, negotiated, and sold.

For Sellers, partnering with a knowledgeable **Listing Agent** has become more critical than ever. In today's transformed market, success depends on an Agent's ability to understand and apply updated regulations, adapt to MLS modifications, and respond to current economic and market trends. This section explores the key roles of Sellers and Listing Agents in this new landscape, highlighting best practices and effective strategies—while building on negotiation insights and compliance guidance discussed in the previous chapter.

A Journey to Success for Real Estate Professionals

Emily stood in the bustling office of her real estate agency, the morning sunlight streaming through the large windows, illuminating her workspace filled with market reports and folders labeled with Clients' names. As a dedicated real estate professional, she understood that each day in this fast-paced industry presented both challenges and opportunities. With the landscape of real estate continually shifting due to economic changes and new regulations, Emily knew that her path to success required a commitment to excellence.

As she prepared to meet with her newest Client—a Seller looking to move into a larger home—Emily paused to reflect on the essential elements that had paved the way for her continued success in real estate.

Professional development remained a cornerstone of her career. She had devoted countless hours to workshops, certifications, and self-improvement courses, ensuring she remained current with industry standards and evolving regulations. This dedication not only kept her skills sharp but also guaranteed that her Clients consistently received informed, high-quality service.

Armed with advanced communication and negotiation skills, Emily had learned to clearly articulate her insights, guiding Clients through complex decisions with confidence. She understood that translating market data and trends into actionable advice was critical in helping Sellers navigate pricing, positioning, and timing. Her market awareness enabled her to identify emerging trends and offer strategic recommendations, empowering her Clients throughout the selling process.

Relationships, Emily knew, were the bedrock of real estate. She had deliberately cultivated a strong professional network by engaging with fellow Agents, lenders, and local business owners. These relationships were more than casual connections—they were strategic partnerships that generated referrals and long-term opportunities, driving sustainable growth in her business.

At the core of Emily's practice was her ability to negotiate effectively. Over the years, she refined a variety of negotiation techniques that allowed her to advocate for her Clients with poise and precision. Whether reviewing offers or managing counter offers, she approached each situation with a solution-focused mindset. Successful negotiations didn't just close deals—they built trust and loyalty, laying the groundwork for repeat business and Client referrals.

In her practice, Emily excessively prioritized Client relationship management. Trust was the foundation of her interactions, and she knew that fostering strong relationships resulted in repeat business and referral ingredients vital for long-term success in real estate. Each interaction was an opportunity to build rapport, whether through face-to-face meetings or virtual check-ins. With the demands of the industry weighing heavily on her, Emily had become proficient in time management. Balancing multiple Clients and transactions required her to prioritize tasks effectively, ensuring that each Client received the attention they deserved while maintaining productivity.

Technology had transformed the real estate landscape, and Emily embraced it wholeheartedly. Leveraging various tools—like CRM software, virtual tours (particularly critical in the new market environment), and digital transaction management she streamlined her operations. The utilization of these technologies not only simplified her workflow but also significantly enhanced the Client experience.

Through it all, Emily understood that adherence to Ethics and Compliance was non-negotiable. Navigating the legal requirements of real estate required diligence and integrity, fostering trust with Clients, and protecting herself from potential liabilities.

Unprecedented Step-By-Step Real Estate Guide

As she glanced at the clock, Emily collected her notes and took a deep breath. It was time to meet her Client. With the knowledge she had gained and the principles she adhered to, she felt confident in her ability to guide this Seller toward a successful transaction. The journey was always evolving, but with each step, she knew she was building not only her career but also trust within her community.

Emily walked toward her Client; she took a moment to reflect on what Sellers typically anticipate during their first meeting with a real estate professional. She understood that this initial interaction could set the tone for their entire relationship, making it crucial for her to meet—and even exceed—their expectations.

Clients often seek empathy and understanding from the very first interaction. They want to feel assured that their real estate Agent genuinely cares about their unique circumstances and goals. Emily reminded herself of the importance of active listening—to truly hear her Client's motivations, concerns, and hopes for their next chapter. This approach would allow her to build rapport and trust from the outset.

Clear communication was another essential element of a successful Client relationship. Clients appreciate it when their Agent articulates the process clearly outlining expected timelines, marketing strategies, and financial considerations in a way that feels accessible and transparent. Emily made it a priority to provide a straightforward overview of the selling journey, ensuring that her Client understood each step and felt empowered to make informed decisions.

In addition, Sellers expect their Agents to be highly knowledgeable about the local market. Emily had spent significant time researching current trends, analyzing data, and staying ahead of neighborhood developments. This market expertise positioned her to offer meaningful insights into comparable listings and strategic pricing. By demonstrating her command of the local real estate landscape, Emily could instill a sense of confidence and assurance in her Client's decision to work with her.

Proactivity was key; Clients wanted to see their Agent take the initiative in marketing their property. Emily had already scheduled professional photos and staged the home for showing, knowing that such details made a difference in attracting potential Buyers. She planned to discuss her marketing strategies during the meeting, revealing her commitment to showcasing the property in the best light possible.

The Sellers would also be seeking a real estate professional who is a skilled negotiator. Clients want assurance that their Agent will fight for their best interests during negotiations. By emphasizing her negotiation techniques and past successes, Emily aimed to reassure her Clients that they were in capable hands when it came time to attract offers and discuss terms.

Finally, Clients appreciated an Agent who could guide them through the emotional journey of selling a home. For many Sellers, parting with a property filled with memories can be a bittersweet experience. Emily aimed to approach this aspect with sensitivity, providing support and understanding throughout the process.

As Emily reached the designated meeting area, she felt a renewed sense of purpose. She was ready to embody all the qualities her Clients anticipated, fostering a relationship built on trust, communication, and shared goals. This first meeting was not just about selling a house; it was about understanding her Client's story and helping them move forward on their journey with confidence.

Emily took a deep breath, adjusted her blazer, and confidently approached her Client, ready to embark on this exciting venture together.

The Role of the Listing Agent: A Guide for Sellers

Before diving into the details of the Settlement, Sellers must understand the pivotal role of the Listing Agent and what they can expect throughout the selling process. Emily, a dedicated Agent, had meticulously prepared a Step-by-Step Guide to Success to ensure her Clients felt informed and confident every step of the way.

As Emily met with Lisa, the Seller, she emphasized the importance of transparency and communication. "My goal is to support you in achieving the best outcome for your home sale," Emily said with a reassuring smile. She handed Lisa the guide outlining the major steps in the selling process:

- **Initial Consultation**: Discussing Lisa's goals, timeline, and expectations for the sale.

- **Market Analysis**: Providing a detailed analysis of comparable properties and current market conditions to help set an appropriate asking price.

- **Home Preparation**: Advising on necessary repairs, staging tips, and enhancements to make the home as appealing as possible to potential Agents.

- **Marketing Strategy**: Outlining a customized marketing strategy that includes professional photography, online Listings, open houses, and targeted advertising.

- **Showings and Open Houses**: Coordinating showings and open houses to attract Buyers and Buyer's Agents, while ensuring that Lisa is informed of any updates.

- **Negotiation**: Representing Lisa in negotiations with potential Buyer's to secure the best price and terms for her home.

- **Closing Process**: Guiding Lisa through the paperwork and logistics involved in closing the sale, ensuring a smooth transition to the next chapter of her life.

Emily also introduced to her Sellers her:

Pledge of Performance – the Duties to Sellers/Clients. As The Listing/Selling Agent Emily:

- will protect and promote their Client's interests while treating all parties honestly.
- will refrain from exaggeration, misrepresentation, or concealment of pertinent facts related to property or transactions.
- will cooperate with other real estate professionals to advance their Clients' best interests.
- When buying or selling on their account or for their families or firms, it will make their true position or interest known.
- do not provide professional services where they have any present or contemplated interest in the property without disclosing that interest to all affected parties.
- will disclose any fee or financial benefit they may receive from recommending related real estate products or services.
- will accept compensation from only one party, except where they make full disclosure to all parties and receive informed consent from their Client.
- will keep the funds of Buyer's make a deposit in a separate escrow account.
- will make sure that details of agreements are spelled out in writing whenever possible and that parties receive copies.

Real Estate Professionals' Duties to the Public:

- Real Estate Professionals will give equal professional service to all Clients and customers irrespective of race, color, religion, sex, disability, familial status, national origin, sexual orientation, or gender identity. Real Estate Professionals do not discriminate in their employment practices.

- Real Estate Professionals are knowledgeable and competent in the fields of practice in which they engage, or they get assistance from a knowledgeable professional or disclose any lack of expertise to their Client.

- Real Estate Professionals are honest and truthful in their communications and present a true picture in their advertising, marketing, and other public representations.

- Real Estate Professionals do not engage in the unauthorized practice of law.

- Real Estate Professionals willingly participate in ethics investigations and enforcement actions.

Real Estate Professionals are committed to transparency, communication, and results. She described her dedication to Client satisfaction, noting that Lisa would always receive timely updates and support throughout the process. This pledge reinforced Lisa's confidence in her decision to partner with Emily, who was committed to acting in her best interest.

With the groundwork laid, Emily then turned to the recent legal changes that would impact Lisa as a Seller. "Now, let's talk about what the real estate Settlement means for you," Emily began.

Lisa listened intently as Emily described the following changes:

- **Specific and Conspicuous Disclosure of Compensation**: The Settlement required that Lisa be provided with clear information regarding the compensation Emily, as the Seller's Agent would receive and how that figure was determined. This change was significant, as it aimed to eliminate confusion and highlight transparency in financial arrangements.

- **Buyer's Agent Written Agreement**: In any situation where compensation was negotiated before the first showing, a Buyer's Agent Written Agreement would now need to be completed in full and signed by the Buyer's Agent and presented to the Seller's Agent. This requirement assured Lisa that all agreements would be documented upfront.

- **Objective Compensation Structures**: Lisa learned that the new rules mandated compensation be presented in objective terms, such as "$0, X flat fee, X percent (%), or X hourly rate." Open-ended compensation phrases like "Agent Broker compensation shall be whatever the amount the Seller is offering" were no longer allowed. This clarity offered peace of mind as Lisa considered how Listing Agents would be compensated. Emily explained during this process that by providing compensation to the Buyer's Agent, Emily would convey this information to many Buyers Broker's, helping to attract Buyer Agent's ready to buy.

- **Prohibition on Excessive Compensation**: A notable new stipulation was that Agents could not receive compensation for brokerage services from any source that exceeded the agreed written rate outlined in the contract. This ensured that Lisa wouldn't face unexpected fees or surprises down the line.

- **Negotiability of Broker Fees**: Finally, the Settlement made it clear that Broker fees and compensation were fully negotiable and not determined by law. Understanding this, empowered Lisa to engage in discussions about her Agent's compensation, knowing she had the freedom to negotiate terms that aligned with her needs.

With this newfound understanding of the Settlement and the proactive guidance from her Listing Agent, Lisa felt more prepared to embark on her selling journey. Equipped with knowledge and trust, she was ready to take the next steps with confidence, knowing that her real estate professional was committed to her success.

Listing Agent Services: A Step-by-Step Guide to Success

Real estate professionals are more than guides; they are dedicated advocates for Sellers. Here's how they add value at every stage of the journey:

- **Understanding Needs**: The Selling Agent begins by learning about the Seller's goals. It is most important to understand the Seller's High Price and Low Price. This keeps both the Seller and Agent working towards the goal and knowing the budget needs of the Seller. Additional preferences that must be understood include the Seller's budget, and priorities, ensuring every property viewed aligns with their goals.
- **Market Expertise**: Agents leverage their knowledge of local market trends, recent sales, and property values to identify the best opportunities.
- **Accessing Listings**: With MLS access, Agents provide tailored property searches, delivering a curated list of homes that match the Seller's home criteria.
- **Arranging Showings**: Agents coordinate tours of the property, both in-person and virtual, accommodating the Seller's schedule and preferences.

- **Negotiation Excellence**: Once the Buyer Agent finds the dream home, the Buyer's Agent references and works with the Seller's Agent. The Seller's Agent works toward achieving the Seller's goal while negotiating terms, price, and contingencies to secure the best deal.
- **Guidance on Inspections and Appraisals**: The Agent arranges and interprets property inspections and appraisals, ensuring the Seller understands the home's condition and value.
- **Contract Expertise**: Real estate professionals prepare and review contracts, ensuring every term is in the Seller's best interest when they are Listing.
- **Closing Support**: From coordinating with title companies to finalizing paperwork, the Agent ensures a seamless closing process.

The document on the next page is one that was crafted by a real estate professional (Author) and distributed to Listing Clients:

Seller's Agent: Pledge Of Performance To Seller

It is always our pleasure to work for YOU! We are committed to preparing you to be an educated Seller. We will:

- Always provide the most vital information available on homes sold that are comparable to homes for sale to determine market price;
- Continually keep you aware of changes in the real estate market;
- Arrange tours of areas, schools, and key points of interest to provide information to Buyers;
- Provide resources upon request regarding neighborhood info, municipal services, schools, churches, etc.;
- Provide resources regarding applicable zoning and building restrictions Seller MUST disclose all known facts about property - a change made as a result of the Settlement;
- Gather up-to-date data on values, taxes, utility costs, etc.;
- Assist in evaluating strengths and weaknesses of property;
- Explain forms, contracts, escrow, and Settlement procedures provide resources for mortgage applications and processing procedures.

We are committed to SAVING YOUR TIME. We will:

- Immediately provide customizable access to MLS-listed properties;
- Identify homes that share similar characteristics as the listed home;
- Provide resources for qualified attorneys, home inspectors, and other service providers;
- Arrange and attend necessary property inspections.

We are committed to helping you sell your home at the best value. We will:

- Prepare studies of property values;

- Perform market analysis on chosen properties;
- Verify that Agents have received resources and have begun discussion with the Lender.

We are committed to YOU - our Seller. We will do all this plus:
- Keep your personal information confidential at all times;
- Educate and explain all aspects of compensation that were outlined in the real estate Settlement on November 26, 2024. Seller can negotiate the compensation amount to be paid, and Seller's Agent is trained in negotiation;
- Coordinate all aspects of the sale and closing;
- Receive compensation ONLY when we have successfully closed your transaction.

To Achieve Best Practices for Compliance:

Emily will share detailed checklists to ensure all new disclosure requirements are met. To accomplish this, listed below are approximately 180 tasks/services performed by real estate professionals. Details regarding negotiation and compensation can be found at the end of activities. This list is a great way to help Listing Agent and Seller with negotiation and compensation. With current and factual information the Listing Agent could review and identify their Seller's needs while negotiating the compensation.

Pre-Listing Activities
- Make an appointment with Seller for Listing presentation;
- Send Seller a written or e-mail confirmation of Listing appointment and call to confirm;
- Review pre-appointment questions;

- Research all comparable currently listed properties;
- Research "Average Days on Market" for this property of this type, price range, and location;
- Download and review property tax roll information;
- Prepare "Comparable Market Analysis" (CMA) to establish fair market value;
- Obtain a copy of the subdivision plat/complex layout;
- Research property ownership & deed type;
- Research property public record information for lot size & dimensions;
- Research and verify legal description;
- Research land use coding and deed restrictions;
- Research property's current use and zoning;
- Verify legal names of owner(s) in the county's public property records;
- Prepare the Listing presentation package with the above materials;
- Perform exterior "Curb Appeal Assessment" of the subject property;
- Compile and assemble formal files on the property;
- Confirm current public schools and explain the impact of schools on market value;
- Review the Listing appointment checklist to ensure all steps and actions have been completed to present the Listing Appointment Presentation;
- Give Seller an overview of current market conditions and projections;
- Review Agents and company's credentials and accomplishments in the market;

- Present the company's profile and position or "niche" in the marketplace;
- Present CMA Results To Seller, including Comparable Sold, Current Listings & Expired;
- Offer pricing strategy based on professional judgment and interpretation of current market conditions;

Discuss and establish Seller's Goals to market effectively:
- Explain the market power and benefits of Multiple Listing Service;
- Explain the market power of web marketing, IDX, and other Webs used;
- Explain the work the Brokerage and Agent do "behind the scenes" and the Agent's availability on weekends;
- Explain the Agent's role in taking calls to screen for qualified Agents and protect Seller from curiosity seekers;
- Present and discuss strategic goals and marketing plan;
- Explain different agency relationships and determine the Seller's preference;
- Review and explain all clauses in the Listing Contract & Addendum and obtain Seller's signature.

Once the Property is entered in MLS using Listing Agreement:
- Review current title information on property appraiser web site;
- Measure overall and heated/cooled square footage;
- Measure interior room sizes;
- Confirm lot size via owner's copy of the certified survey, if available;
- Note any unrecorded property lines, agreements, and easements;

- Obtain house plans, if applicable and available and review house plans;
- Order plat map (if required by Lender) for retention in Listing file;
- Prepare showing instructions for Buyer's Agents and agree on showing time window with Seller;
- Obtain current mortgage loan(s) information: companies and loan account numbers;
- Verify current loan information with lender(s) to determine if the loan (s) is assumable and any special requirements;
- Review current appraisal if available;
- Identify the Homeowner Association (HOA) manager if applicable and verify Homeowner Association Fees - mandatory or optional and current annual fee;
- Mandatory to provide a copy of the Homeowner Association bylaws and Seller must sign the receipt of these forms;
- Research electricity provider's name and phone number and calculate average utility usage for last 12 months;
- Water System: Calculate average water fees or rates for last 12 months;
- Verify the city sewer/septic tank system;
- Inquire if the Seller has roof solar panels, and if there is a monthly payment for these;
- Well Water: Confirm well status, depth, and output from the Well Report;
- Natural Gas: Research/verify availability and supplier's name and phone number;
- Verify security system, current term of service, and whether owned or leased;

- Ascertain the need for lead-based paint disclosure (Homes built prior to 1978 likely used lead paint);
- Prepare a detailed list of property amenities and assess market impact;
- Prepare a detailed list of property's "Inclusions & Conveyances with Sale" and include with Listing as well as a signed document that Buyer had received the "inventory list" of items;
- Compile a list of complete repairs and maintenance items (these must be included with disclosure);
- Explain the benefits of Homeowner Warranty to Seller;
- Assist Sellers with completion and submission of Homeowner Warranty Application and when received, place Homeowner Warranty in the property file for conveyance at the time of sale;
- Have an extra key made for the lockbox;
- Arrange for installation of yard sign;
- Confirm Seller has completed, and Buyer has signed receipt of Seller's Disclosure form;
- Review results of Curb Appeal Assessment with Seller and provide suggestions to improve sale ability;
- Review results of Interior Décor Assessment and suggest changes to shorten time on the market;
- Load Listing into transaction management software program.

Verify if the property has rental units involved. And if so:
- Make copies of all leases for retention in the Listing file;
- Verify all rents & deposits;
- Send "Vacancy Checklist" to Seller if the property is vacant;
- Inform tenants of the Listing and discuss how showings will be handled.

Prepare MLS Profile Sheet and enter Listing in MLS Database:

- Agents are responsible for "quality control" and accuracy of Listing data and payment amounts are prohibited permanently from being entered in MLS;

- Enter property data from the Profile Sheet into the MLS Listing Database;

- Proofread MLS database Listing for accuracy, including proper placement in mapping function;

- Add property to Seller's Brokerage Active Listings list;

- Provide Seller with signed copies of Listing Agreement and MLS Profile Sheet Data Form within 48 hours.

- Attach all documents that must be completed by the Buyer and submitted with contract to purchase in MLS. These supplements include:
    - ✓ HOA Disclosure
    - ✓ HOA Application
    - ✓ Community for 55+ Disclosure
    - ✓ Flood Disclosure
    - ✓ Housing for Older Persons
    - ✓ Inventory included with purchase of home and others.

Marketing of Property:

- Take additional photos for uploading into MLS and use them in flyers;

- Discuss the efficacy of panoramic photography Marketing The Listing, as well as positive reactions in aerial photos;

- Create and print Internet ads with Seller's permission;

- Coordinate showings with Seller, tenants, and others;

- Communicate with Seller that real estate professionals, return all calls - weekends included;
- Place electronic lock box, once authorized by the owner, on property, programmed with agreed-upon showing time window;
- Prepare mailing and contact list;
- Generate mail-merge letters to contact list;
- Order "Just Listed" labels & reports;
- Prepare flyers & feedback emails;
- Prepare property marketing brochure for Seller's review;
- Arrange for printing or copying of supply of marketing brochures or fliers;
- Send marketing brochures to all company Agent mailboxes or email addresses;
- Upload Listing to company and Agent Internet site;
- Distribute "Just Listed" notice to neighborhood residents;
- Advise Network Referral Program of Listing;
- Provide marketing data for Agents coming through international relocation networks;
- Provide marketing data to Agents coming from referral networks;
- Provide "Special Feature" cards for marketing, and place in home where referenced;
- Submit ads to companies' participating Internet real estate sites;
- If price changes, convey promptly to all Marketing and Internet groups;
- Reprint/supply brochures promptly as needed;
- Feedback e-mails sent to Buyer's Agents after showings;
- Review weekly Market Study;

- Discuss feedback from showing Agents with the Seller to determine if changes will accelerate the sales;
- Place regular weekly update calls to Seller to discuss marketing & pricing;
- Before entering price changes in the MLS Listing database, prepare Market Report, Current Listings Report and Comparable Market Sales to discuss with Seller, and determine price change.

The Offer and Contract

- Receive and review all Offers to Purchase contracts submitted by the Buyer or Buyer's Agent;
- Review comparable MLS Listings regularly to ensure property remains competitive in price, terms, conditions, and availability;
- Evaluate contract offer(s) and area and prepare a "net sheet" on each for the Seller for comparison purposes;
- Counsel Seller on offers. Explain the merits and weaknesses of each component of each contract;
- Contact the Buyer's Agent to review the Buyer's qualifications and discuss the offer;
- Confirm Buyer is pre-qualified by calling the Loan Officer;
- Request Buyer pre-qualification letter from Loan Officer;
- Email copies of the completed contract and all addendums to the closing attorney or title company;
- When the Offer to Purchase Contract is accepted and signed by Seller, deliver to Buyer's Agent;
- Request Buyer's Agent deposit earnest money in the escrow account within 3 days;
- Disseminate "Under-Contract Showing Restrictions" as Seller requests;

- Deliver copies of the fully signed contract to purchase to the Seller;
- Request receipt of Down Payment made by the Agent at an inappropriate time;
- Email copies of the contract to purchase to the Buyer's Agent;
- Email copies of the contract to purchase to the lender;
- Provide copies of the signed contract to purchase for the office file;
- Change status in MLS to "Sale Pending";
- Update transaction management program to show "Sale Pending";
- Review Agent's credit report results -- Advise Seller of worst- and best-case scenarios;
- Provide credit report information to the Seller if the property will be Seller-financed;
- Inquire with lender the Discount Points locked in dates;
- Order septic system inspection, if applicable;
- Receive and review septic system report and assess any possible impact on sale;
- Deliver a copy of the septic system inspection report to Lender & Buyer's Agent;
- Deliver well flow test report copy to lender, Buyer's Agent and property Listing file;
- Verify mold inspection ordered if required.

Tracking the Loan Process
- Confirm verifications of contract deposit and Buyer's employment have been verified;
- Follow loan processing through to the underwriter;

- Add lender and other vendors to transaction management programs so the Buyer's Agent and Seller can track the progress of the sale;
- Contact lender weekly to ensure processing is on track;
- Relay final approval of Buyer's loan application to Seller.

Home Inspection
- Coordinate Buyer's professional home inspection with Seller;
- Review the home inspector's report;
- Enter completion into the transaction management tracking software program;
- Explain Seller's responsibilities concerning loan limits and interpret any clauses in the contract;
- Ensure Seller's compliance with Home Inspection Clause requirements;
- Recommend or assist Seller with identifying and negotiating with trustworthy contractors to perform any required repairs;
- Negotiate payment and oversee completion of all required repairs on Seller's behalf.

The Appraisal
- Schedule Appraisal;
- Follow-Up On Appraisal;
- Enter completion into the transaction management program;
- Assist Seller in questioning the appraisal report if it seems too low;

Closing Preparation:
- Coordinate closing process with Buyer's Agent and lender;
- Confirm Buyer has instructions for closing;
- Update closing forms & files;

- Ensure all parties have all forms and information needed to close the sale;
- Identify the selected location where closing will be held;
- Confirm closing date and time and notify all parties;
- Assist in solving any title problems (boundary disputes, easements, etc.) or in obtaining Death Certificates;

Assist Buyer's Agent:

- Schedule and conduct Final Walk Thru before closing;
- Research all tax, HOA, utility, and other applicable proration;
- Request final closing figures from closing Agent (attorney or title company);
- Receive & carefully review closing figures to ensure the accuracy of preparation;
- Forward verified closing figures to Buyer's Agent;
- Request copy of closing documents from Lender and Attorney or Title Company;
- Confirm Buyer and Buyer's Agent have received title insurance commitment;
- Provide "Homeowners Warranty" for availability at closing;
- Review all closing documents carefully for errors.
- Forward closing documents to the Absentee Seller as requested;
- Confirm earnest money deposit check from escrow account wired to the closing office;
- Coordinate this closing with Seller's next purchase and resolve timing problems;
- Have a "no surprises" closing so that Seller receives net proceeds at closing;

- Refer Sellers to one of the best Agents at their destination, if applicable;
- Change MLS status to Sold;
- In MLS enter the sale date, price, selling Broker and Agent's ID numbers, etc.;
- Closeout Listing in transaction management program;
- Follow Up After Closing;
- Answer questions about filing claims with the Homeowner Warranty company if requested;
- Attempt to clarify and resolve any conflicts about repairs if the Buyer is not satisfied.
- Respond to any follow-on calls and provide any additional information required from office files;
- Mark the First Anniversary sale date to send the Seller and the Buyer a congratulatory note. This is truly essential. Recognizing a positive transaction will be well received if you send a thank you note to the Seller and Buyer on their first month's anniversary, inquiring how they are in their new home, and if there is anyone who would benefit from your great work.

The Comprehensive Role of the Listing Agent

As Lisa reflected on the complexity of selling her home, she gained a renewed appreciation for the expertise her Listing Agent, Emily, would bring to the table. The real estate journey was far from a solo endeavor—it was a collaborative process requiring a wide range of tasks, careful planning, and nuanced market understanding. Lisa recognized that Emily's role extended well beyond simply listing the property; she would be instrumental in orchestrating every step of the transaction to ensure a successful outcome.

Lisa also acknowledged that Emily's compensation should reflect the depth and scope of services provided throughout the listing process.

From the moment they began working together, Emily demonstrated her dedication through pre-listing activities designed to lay a strong foundation. She began by scheduling a comprehensive listing presentation—an in-depth meeting to learn more about Lisa's goals and establish a transparent, step-by-step strategy for the sale. This was followed by detailed research into comparable properties in the area, enabling Emily to deliver a precise and well-supported home valuation tailored to current market conditions.

Comparable Market Analysis (CMA).

Lisa appreciated that Emily's expertise extended far beyond the numbers. She didn't just present a price point—she offered a full picture, including insights into the average days on the market for comparable properties, giving Lisa a clearer understanding of the competitive landscape. Emily meticulously reviewed property tax records, verified the legal description, and confirmed applicable zoning laws—each of which could have a direct impact on pricing and market positioning.

When it came time for the listing presentation, Lisa was impressed by the personalized marketing strategy Emily proposed. The plan included a comprehensive marketing timeline and a master strategy that highlighted the home's best features using the latest digital tools and platforms. Emily's attention to detail stood out, from conducting a Curb Appeal Assessment to offering specific improvement suggestions designed to enhance the home's presentation and market value.

Once the property was officially listed, Emily seamlessly managed the tasks that followed. She prepared show instructions tailored for Buyer's Agents and ensured all required disclosures were accurate and complete. Lisa found great value in Emily's ability to coordinate effectively with key players in the transaction, including appraisers and home inspectors, to streamline the process.

During the negotiation phase, Lisa felt fully supported. Emily carefully reviewed all incoming offers, prepared detailed net sheets to help compare terms, and advocated for Lisa's best interests with professionalism and confidence. Her guidance was instrumental in helping Lisa make informed decisions at every step.

Emily's dedication didn't end once an offer was accepted. She continued to lead through the closing preparations, double-checking documentation and ensuring all parties stayed informed, eliminating last-minute surprises and promoting a smooth closing experience.

Even after the sale, Emily's service remained ongoing. Lisa appreciated the thoughtful follow-up approach Emily embraced—checking in after the move and remaining available as a trusted resource. It was clear that, for Emily, real estate wasn't just about transactions—it was about relationships.

Lisa understood how invaluable it was to have someone like Emily guiding her through the complexities of selling a home. From the earliest planning stages to the final signatures—and beyond—Emily's comprehensive approach made the process feel manageable, strategic, and deeply personal. With a dedicated professional at her side, Lisa felt empowered and ready for the next chapter in her journey.

Explaining the Compensation Negotiation Process to the Seller

As the landscape of real estate evolves, understanding the new compensation structures has become essential for Sellers navigating the complexities of property transactions. For Lisa, embarking on the journey of selling her home, it was crucial to grasp how these changes would affect her negotiating power and overall experience. With Emily, her Listing Agent, beside her, they prepared to delve into the nuances of the compensation negotiation process.

Understanding the New Compensation Structure

Compensation structure in real estate has shifted towards enhanced flexibility and transparency, a welcome change for Sellers. Whether you're new to the process or a seasoned Seller, knowing how to negotiate compensation is critical to achieving favorable terms.

Direct Negotiation with the Seller

This approach allows for compensation to be negotiated directly between the Buyer and Seller as part of the home-buying process. As Lisa and Emily discussed, when a Buyer finds a home they wish to purchase, the Buyer's Agent may propose their compensation as part of the overall offer to the Seller. This negotiation often influences not just the compensation rate but also the purchase price and other terms of the sale.

For instance, if the Buyer's Agent proposes a lower compensation rate, the Buyer might increase their purchase offer to entice the Seller to agree to the terms. Understanding this dynamic enabled Lisa to appreciate how the negotiations could shape the outcome of her sale.

Pre-negotiated compensation with the Buyer's Agent

Alternatively, Lisa learned that she and Emily could agree on a compensation structure before any show took place. This proactive strategy ensures both parties are on the same page when it comes to compensation, creating clarity from the outset. By discussing and establishing a compensation rate or fee that would remain in place regardless of the Buyer's offer, Lisa felt a sense of security and transparency—there would be no surprises when it came to how compensations were handled.

Ensuring Positive Experience

To ensure a smooth and successful selling experience, Lisa recognized the importance of taking a thoughtful, informed approach. Together with Emily, she focused on the following key steps:

Educate Yourself: Lisa understood that becoming familiar with the basics of negotiation and recent industry changes was essential. She felt empowered to ask Emily questions whenever she encountered terms or processes that were unclear. Staying informed gave her greater confidence throughout the transaction.

Choose the Right Agent: Finding an agent who was not only experienced but also compatible with her communication style was a top priority. Lisa chose Emily because she felt heard, understood, and respected. Emily provided transparent guidance on fees and services from the start— qualities that proved invaluable throughout the negotiation process.

Discuss Compensation Early: Transparency in compensation was non-negotiable. Lisa and Emily made it a point to address expectations early, ensuring that both parties were aligned. Establishing a clear plan helped prevent any future misunderstandings and set a professional tone for their collaboration.

Negotiate Effectively: Lisa remained open-minded and flexible, understanding that compensation discussions could be integrated into the broader negotiation strategy. She trusted Emily to advocate on her behalf with both professionalism and finesse, knowing her Agent was fully committed to achieving the best possible outcome.

Focusing on Value

Lisa also recognized that focusing solely on obtaining the lowest compensation wasn't necessarily the best approach. Quality service from a skilled Agent like Emily saved her time and money, ultimately ensuring a smooth transaction. Emily's extensive knowledge and dedication meant Lisa was not just a number but a valued Client.

Positive Experience in Action With Emily's help, Lisa imagined the process unfolding smoothly. They agreed on a compensation rate upfront and some ideas if the Buyer's Agent requested compensation assistance, effectively eliminating any future uncertainty. During negotiations, Emily would advocate fiercely on Lisa's behalf, keeping her informed at every step of the way. This proactive approach stripped the stress away from the transaction, instead creating a rewarding home-selling experience.

Industry-Wide Changes and Their Impact on Agents

The recent Settlement brought substantial changes to real estate practices, affecting not only transactions but also how Buyer's and Seller's Agents operate:

Greater Transparency in Transactions: It is the responsibility of Buyer's and Seller's Agents to disclose compensation structures and fees more explicitly, including negotiation training to facilitate agreement between Sellers and Buyers.

Changes in Compensation Negotiation: The Settlement emphasized the need for flexibility and clarity in compensation discussions, encouraging Buyer and Seller Agents to justify their rates with detailed descriptions of services.

Increased Focus on Ethical Practices: Ethics have become central to real estate transactions, with Buyer and Seller Agents now focusing more on compliance with updated guidelines to promote fairness.

Impact on MLS Operations: Changes necessitated compliance with new Listing policies, enhancing consumer access to real estate Listings and Buyer's Agents to adapt their strategies accordingly.

Empowered Consumers: Today, consumers have greater access to information, allowing them more control over transactions. Agents must adjust their approaches to accommodate well-informed Clients and ensure comprehensive consultations.

The Recap of Selling Your Home

Conclusion: The National Association's Settlement has ushered in a new era in the real estate industry—one defined by transparency, ethical practices, and increased consumer empowerment. For real estate professionals, this transformation demands adaptability, continuous skill development, and a renewed focus on delivering exceptional service to all Clients.

As Lisa discovered through her eyes, navigating this updated landscape can empower Sellers with a clearer understanding of their options and greater confidence in their decisions. With the right support and knowledge, you, too, can approach the home-selling process with assurance and clarity.

If you have questions or need additional guidance, don't hesitate to reach out to your local real estate board, state association, or the National Association. Expert assistance is available to help you make informed, empowered decisions every step of the way.

Chapter 6

How a Buyer represented by a Buyer's Agent Accomplishes a Successful Journey to Homeownership

A Journey to Homeownership: Understanding the Written Buyer Agreement

One afternoon, Sarah met with Jake, her trusted real estate Agent, at a cozy coffee shop filled with the comforting aroma of freshly brewed coffee. Her heart fluttered with anticipation as they sat down to discuss her dream of owning a home.

Their conversation began with excitement, but soon turned to something critical—the Written Buyer Agreement.

Jake leaned in slightly, his tone calm and reassuring. "This agreement isn't just another piece of paperwork," he said. "It's our shared roadmap for your home-buying journey."

Sarah tilted her head, curiosity sparking in her eyes. "Why do I need it?"

Jake smiled. "Think of it like going on an adventure without a map. You might know where you want to end up, but without clear directions, the journey gets confusing. The Written Buyer Agreement gives us structure. It outlines expectations, protects your interests, and ensures we're on the same page every step of the way."

As Jake continued, Sarah began to understand that the agreement served more than one purpose.

"First," Jake said, "it clearly defines my role as your Buyer Agent. I'll be responsible for finding homes that match your needs, negotiating offers on your behalf, and guiding you through every step. Having all of this in writing ensures we both know what to expect."

"So, it also protects me?" Sarah asked, her understanding deepening.

"Correct!" Jake replied, his enthusiasm unmistakable. "It sets the foundation for trust and transparency. You'll know upfront what services I'm providing and how I'll be compensated. That clarity helps build a strong, supportive relationship."

As they reviewed the agreement together, Jake patiently walked Sarah through each section. He explained how Agent compensation typically works: "This document allows us to spell out the negotiated compensation, whether it's a flat fee, hourly fee, or a percentage, and whether it's paid by the Seller or by you, the Buyer. It's negotiable, and it's important you're fully informed."

They also discussed ways to customize the agreement to fit Sarah's needs, including the timeframe of their working relationship and her specific preferences. This collaborative approach reassured Sarah that her comfort and goals were always a priority.

With the agreement signed, Sarah felt empowered and ready to begin the exciting journey of finding her perfect home. As she and Jake browsed listings together, one cozy house stood out. It felt just right.

While touring the property, Sarah realized how much the Written Buyer Agreement had strengthened her confidence. It wasn't just a document— it was a foundation. Through her discussions with Jake, she gained clarity and negotiation skills that helped her move forward with certainty.

In the end, Sarah successfully closed on her dream home, grateful for the partnership she had built with Jake. The Written Buyer Agreement had turned what could have been an overwhelming experience into a guided, rewarding adventure, rooted in trust, transparency, and collaboration.

As they celebrated the successful closing, Sarah reflected on how far she had come. With knowledge in hand and support at her side, she felt truly prepared to navigate the complex world of real estate, confident in the advocacy she had received every step of the way.

What Are Real Estate Professionals?

In the bustling world of real estate, professionals like Emily are far more than facilitators of transactions—they are strategic partners committed to guiding clients through every step of the buying or selling process. With market expertise, strong negotiation skills, and comprehensive administrative support, real estate Agents bring clarity and confidence to what can often feel like an overwhelming journey.

For Buyers, especially, the path to homeownership can be filled with uncertainty. That's why having a knowledgeable Agent in their corner makes all the difference.

"Always feel free to ask your Agent for more details," Emily would often remind her Clients, reinforcing that her job wasn't just about closing deals—it was about empowering and supporting them at every stage.

Buyer Agent Services: A Step-by-Step Guide to Success

- Real estate professionals act as devoted advocates for Buyers, providing invaluable services at every stage of the home-buying journey.

- **Understanding Needs**: Emily began each relationship by diving deep into her Clients' preferences, budgets, and priorities. During their initial consultation, she asked targeted questions to ensure that every property they viewed aligned with their goals. "We'll also discuss the necessary Written Buyer Agreement," she explained, "as well as the options for negotiating your Buyer's Agent compensation." This openness laid the groundwork for a trusting partnership.

- **Market Expertise**: Armed with extensive knowledge of local market trends and recent sales, Emily helped her Buyers identify the best opportunities. "It's crucial to understand the market," she would say. "Let's find the perfect home that offers both value and comfort for you."

- **Accessing Listings**: Utilizing her membership in the Multiple Listing Service (MLS), Emily provided tailored property searches for her Clients, delivering curated lists of homes that met their criteria. "With the MLS, we can explore a variety of options to find the best fit," she often assured her Clients.

- **Schedule Showings**: Coordinating property tours was another vital service. Emily ensured that showings were convenient for her Buyers, accommodating their schedules for both in-person and virtual tours. "I want this process to be as enjoyable and stress-free as possible," she noted, showcasing her commitment to their experience.

- **Negotiation Excellence**: Once a potential home was identified, Emily's negotiation prowess came into play. "We'll negotiate terms, price, and contingencies to secure the best possible deal for you," she promised. Her Clients felt confident knowing that they had an advocate on their side, fighting for their best interests.

- **Guidance on Inspections and Appraisals**: Throughout the process, Emily arranged for property inspections and appraisals, assisting her Clients in interpreting the findings. "Understanding the home's condition and market value is essential," she would remind them, ensuring Buyers were informed about the property they were considering.

- **Navigating Financing**: To simplify the financial aspect of buying a home, Emily connected her Clients with trusted lenders and Credit Unions to explore various financing options. "Let's identify down payment or closing cost assistance programs that can help ease your financial burden," she suggested, taking a proactive approach to her Clients' needs.

- **Contract Expertise**: As the transaction progressed, Emily prepared and reviewed contracts, ensuring that all terms aligned with her Buyers' interests. Her attention to detail gave them peace of mind as they moved forward.

- **Closing Support**: Emily coordinated with Attorneys or Title companies, finalized paperwork, and ensured a seamless closing process. "I'll be here every step of the way, making sure nothing slips through the cracks," she reassured her Clients, further solidifying their trust in her expertise.

Navigating Compensation and Negotiations

In today's real estate landscape, Agent compensation is no longer guaranteed, making proactive communication more important than ever. Emily always addressed compensation openly with her clients, ensuring clarity about both her rates and the specific services she provided. "We need to be clear about financial arrangements," she would say, "and negotiate what works best for everyone involved."

Fostering an atmosphere that welcomed negotiation was vital to Emily's approach. She encouraged her Clients to confidently engage in these discussions, knowing that informed, collaborative conversations often led to the most successful outcomes.

"Negotiation is at the heart of every real estate transaction," she explained. "And being prepared makes all the difference."

By emphasizing transparency and mutual benefit, Emily created a collaborative environment that supported a positive experience for all parties. In doing so, she embodied the true spirit of a real estate professional—an advocate fully invested in her Clients' success.

Explaining the Commission Negotiation Process to Buyers

In the ever-evolving world of real estate, compensation structures have shifted toward greater flexibility and transparency. For First Time Home Buyers like Sarah, this change brought not only more options but also the confidence to navigate the process with clarity.

As Sarah began her homeownership journey, her Agent, Jake, ensured she understood the importance of discussing commission upfront. "Whether it's your first time buying or your fifth," Jake said as they sat in their favorite local coffee shop, "knowing how to negotiate compensation gives you control and confidence."

Direct Negotiation with the Seller

Jake introduced the first direct negotiation approach between the Buyer and Seller.

"In this process," he explained, "my compensation is negotiated as part of your overall offer to the Seller. We'll agree on the amount or percentage together before submitting the offer."

Sarah leaned in, intrigued. Jake continued, illustrating how it would work in practice.

"Let's say you find a home you love," he said. "As part of the offer, I'll include my compensation terms. That can affect the purchase price or other parts of the deal, so we'll make sure it's structured in a way that supports your goals."

Pre-negotiated commission with the Buyer's Agent

Jake then introduced another option: pre-negotiated compensation with the Buyer's Agent.

"Alternatively," he said, "we can agree on a compensation structure before we even begin touring homes. That way, everything's clear from the start."

He leaned in slightly, making sure Sarah understood. "Think of it this way—before we view any properties, we'll decide on my compensation, regardless of what the Seller offers. That way, there are no surprises later on."

Sarah nodded, reassured by the idea of having clear expectations in place from the very beginning.

Ensuring a Positive Experience:

- Jake emphasized that a positive home-buying experience hinged on proactive communication and preparation.

Educate Yourself:

- "It's essential to familiarize yourself with the basics of real estate negotiation and the recent industry changes," Jake advised. He encouraged Sarah to ask questions whenever she felt uncertain about terms or processes, assuring her that it was always okay to seek clarification.

Choose the Right Agent:

- "Compatibility matters," Jake noted as he pointed to the importance of selecting an Agent who communicated effectively and understood her unique needs. "Make sure your Agent is upfront about their fees and services and has experience negotiating under the new compensation structures."

Discuss Compensation Early:

- "Transparency is key here," Jake stated. By discussing compensation expectations at the beginning of their relationship, they could create a solid foundation that would help avoid misunderstandings later. "I suggest we consider a pre-agreed compensation rate," he added.

Negotiate Effectively:

- Jake encouraged Sarah to be flexible when negotiating compensation as part of the offer to the Seller. "Trust my expertise as your Agent to guide you through this process," he reassured her.

Focus on Value:

- Finally, he highlighted that focusing solely on the lowest compensation wasn't the best strategy. "Quality service matters. A skilled Agent saves you time and money, ensuring a smooth transaction."

As they wrapped up their meeting, Sarah felt empowered and informed, ready to dive into the home-buying journey ahead. With Jake by her side, she was confident in her ability to navigate the complexities of negotiation and feel in control of the process.

Positive Experience in Action

Picture yourself beginning your home-buying journey with an experienced real estate Agent fully invested in your success. From the first conversation, they clearly explained the updated compensation structure, ensuring you know what to expect. Together, you agree on a fair compensation rate upfront, eliminating the uncertainty that often complicates negotiations.

Throughout the process, your Agent advocates on your behalf with skill and dedication. Their proactive communication keeps you informed at every step, creating a transparent, collaborative environment. With each conversation, you gain a deeper appreciation for the value your Agent brings—not just in closing deals, but in guiding you confidently through every decision.

By educating yourself about the process, selecting the right Agent, and approaching compensation discussions with clarity and flexibility, you position yourself to navigate the complexities of home buying with confidence. This empowered mindset turns what might have felt overwhelming into a rewarding opportunity for success.

Industry-Wide Changes and Their Impact on Agents

The recent Settlement from the National Association has ushered in significant changes to real estate practices, reshaping the landscape for Agents and their operations. These shifts have a wide-reaching impact on how they engage with Clients and navigate the evolving market.

Greater Transparency in Transactions

- **Impact**: Agents are now required to disclose compensation structures and fees more openly. This increased transparency is crucial, as it fosters trust and clarity in Client-Agent relationships.

- **Practice Change**: Agents are undergoing negotiation training to enhance their ability to guide Clients effectively through discussions about compensation, helping reach mutually beneficial agreements.

Changes in Commission Negotiation

- **Impact**: The Settlement has altered the way Agents discuss and negotiate compensation, emphasizing flexibility and transparency to adapt to the new norms.

- **Practice Change**: Agents may need to justify their compensation rates by providing detailed descriptions of their services and exploring alternative pricing models to fit consumer needs.

Increased Focus on Ethical Practices

- **Impact**: Ethics have become a cornerstone of real estate transactions, elevating the standards to which Agents must adhere.

- **Practice Change**: Agents are required to undergo ethics training and comply with updated guidelines, ensuring fair practices and promoting a higher level of integrity within the industry.

Impact on MLS Operations

- **Impact**: MLS policies have adapted to comply with the Settlement terms, changing how Listings are shared and accessed, thus enhancing consumer information flow.

- **Practice Change**: Agents must adjust to new MLS rules, focusing on enhancing consumer access to Listings and utilizing innovative ways to market properties.

Empowered Consumers

- **Impact**: With greater access to information, consumers now possess more control over their transactions. This knowledge enables Clients to make informed decisions as they navigate the Buying or Selling process.

- **Practice Change**: Agents must adjust their strategies to accommodate informed Clients, often requiring more detailed consultations and discussions that prioritize the Clients' understanding of the process.

Through these industry-wide changes, real estate professionals are better equipped to foster empowering relationships with their Clients, ensuring that consumers have access to the information and support they need to thrive in an ever-evolving marketplace.

Buyer/Client Benefits of Working with a Real Estate Professional:

The relationship between a Buyer and a real estate professional is built on trust, transparency, and shared goals. With the right Agent by your side, you gain access to invaluable expertise, dedicated advocacy, and a wealth of resources to guide you through the home-buying process.

The Real Estate Professional's Commitment According to the National Association of Realtors:

"When working with a Buyer, a real estate professional has a duty under the Code of Ethics and MLS policy to make their Buyer aware of all listings that meet their specifications—including those without an offer of compensation."

This commitment ensures that Buyers remain fully informed and supported at every stage of their journey, reinforcing the Agent's role as a true advocate, not just a facilitator.

Conclusion

In conclusion, real estate professionals play a pivotal role in guiding clients through the property transaction process. From navigating market complexities to negotiating favorable terms, they provide the support and expertise Buyers and Sellers need to make confident, informed decisions.

By fostering open communication about compensation and utilizing clear, written agreements, Buyers can build strong, productive relationships with their Agents. Engaging in proactive discussions—especially in light of the new forms introduced through the National

Association settlement—empowers Clients to negotiate terms that align with their goals and financial expectations.

Whether purchasing a first home or making a strategic investment, Buyers benefit immensely from the advocacy, insight, and experience a skilled real estate professional provides. As the industry continues to evolve, especially under the influence of recent policy changes, transparency and trust remain the cornerstones of effective partnerships.

Ultimately, the National Association of Settlement marks a transformative shift in the real estate landscape—one that promotes greater clarity around compensation and strengthens the Agent/Client relationship. By embracing these changes and making informed choices, Buyers are better equipped to navigate the real estate market with confidence and success.

And a greater emphasis on ethical behavior. Real estate professionals will adapt to these changes by embracing new practices, enhancing their skills, and focusing on providing exceptional service to meet the evolving expectations of consumers.

These are examples of the focus a Buyer has when they make their professional real estate Agent selection. It will help you understand what an Agent does on your behalf.

Buyer's Agent will:

Introduce you to an essential new topic: the Written Buyer Agreement. "This agreement," Jake explained, leaning closer, "is not just more paperwork; it's our roadmap to navigate your home-buying journey together." The Buyer's Agent will;

- Not enter any compensation in the MLS

- Complete the Written Buyer Broker Agreement and complete it before touring a home

- The compensation for the Buyer's Agent will include the compensation amount.

- Always provide the most available vital information on prospective homes;

- Continually keep Buyers aware of changes in the real estate market;

- Arrange tours of areas, schools, and key points of interest as requested;

- Resources regarding neighborhood info, municipal services, schools, churches, etc. Upon request;

- Zoning and building restrictions upon request;

- Disclose all known facts about properties and provide disclosures;

- Assist in evaluating the strengths and weaknesses of the property;

- Explain forms, contracts, escrow, and Settlement procedures;

- Provide resources for mortgage applications and processing procedures.

Buyer's Agent is committed to SAVING YOUR TIME. Your Agent will:

- Immediately   provide customizable access to MLS-listed properties;

- Assist as needed on all unlisted properties;

- Show homes only in the price range as directed by your financial situation;

- Provide resources for qualified attorneys, home inspectors, and other service providers;

- Arrange and attend necessary property inspections.

Your Agent is committed to helping you find the best value and will:

- Prepare studies of property values and perform market analysis;

- Provide resources and begin discussion for financing options;

- Explore all down payment and closing cost assistance programs.

- Write and present all contracts to the Seller;

- Always negotiate on the Client's behalf.

We are committed to YOU - the Buyer. Your Agent will do all this plus:

- Keep your personal information confidential at all times.

- Coordinate all aspects of the sale and closing;

- Be reimbursed with compensation ONLY when we have successfully closed your transaction.

On the following pages, you will find forms and checklists created by the author and used in Business. Buyer or Seller, and all real estate professionals, you may use this information in any way that results in success.

Client's Pledge Of Performance To Buyer

It is always our pleasure to work for YOU! We are committed to providing honest information and preparing you to be an educated Buyer. We are **committed to assisting you with:**

- An objective compensation structure (e.g., a fixed fee or percentage), rather than an open-ended statement based on the Seller's offer.

- Term limiting the Agent's compensation to the agreed-upon rate within the agreement.

- A clear statement that Broker fees and compensation are fully negotiable and not mandated by law;

- Written agreements are required for both in-person and virtual tours;

- No written agreement is necessary if you are merely inquiring at an open house.

- While a Seller may offer compensation to the Buyer's Agent, this offer cannot be shared on MLS;

- You can still accept concessions from the Seller, such as covering closing costs;

- The Buyer's Agent will explain and help the Buyer complete and sign the agreement with the Agent before touring homes;

- The agreement outlines compensation terms, ensures transparency, and establishes the services the Agent provides.

Compensation Disclosure:

- The disclosure will provide the exact amount or rate of Buyer's Agent compensation.

- This fosters trust and ensures Buyers understand their financial obligations.

Seller Compensation Offers:

- Seller can offer compensation to Buyer's Agent but can no longer be displayed on the MLS.

- Arrangements are privately negotiated or marketed through other channels, and the Buyer is informed of all that is accomplished.

Enhance Buyer Flexibility:

- Buyer has greater control over how the Agent is compensated, with options to negotiate directly with the Seller or include Agent fees in purchase offers.

EXCLUSIVE BUYER AGREEMENT

It is always our pleasure to work for YOU!

We will provide you with the following services:

- Help you prepare a comprehensive budget for the home purchase. In addition, we will explain how a Buyer/Agent can/will be compensated and the total amount of compensation. The details of the negotiation and a full explanation of the Written Buyer Agreement, which requires the Buyer's signature, will be provided, and the Buyer will have unlimited time for questions.

- Resources will be provided that will assist you in securing the best financial program for your specific situation with the lowest interest rate and least expensive closing costs. We will then have a pre-approval certificate generated to give you the best competitive advantage in future negotiations. In addition, we will write a letter to the Seller indicating why choosing you as the Buyer is in their best interest!

- We will research with you on any possible down payment or closing cost assistance.

- We will provide you with regular updates from our Buyer profiling system of all the new Listings that match your criteria. This will allow you to drive by and determine which properties you want to see.

- We will do our best to arrange a private showing of any home you want to see including new construction and For Sale by Owner properties.

- We will discuss strategies when you find a home you like regarding offer price, financing terms, interest rate, possession date, and anything else you want to know.

- We will help you prepare the offer with the terms, provisions, and addendums weighted in your best interest.

- We will present the offer on your behalf and negotiate in your favor to help you secure the property at the best possible price and terms.

- We will help coordinate your total home purchase: home inspection, termite inspection, and appraisal, homeowners' insurance flood insurance when needed, and title insurance.

- We will communicate and coordinate your closing between the Lender, Listing Agent, other vendors, and Attorney or Title company.

You agree to:

- Seek pre-approval from a home lender before viewing property.

- Notify us of any homes you wish to view, such as For Sale by Owners, or builders, that you have informed that a professional Agent will represent you.

- Formulate any offer on any home (new or resale) through us.

- Understand that you are not under any obligation at any time to buy or build a home.

- Understand that this agreement expires one year from today's date.

- Acknowledge that the real estate professional is being retained solely as a Real Estate Agent and not as an attorney, engineer, home inspector, or any other professional service provider.

- Consulting with legal counsel or an accountant is a choice that you may make at any time.

Understanding the Legal Written Buyer Agreement:

As Sarah embarked on her exciting journey to find her first home, she recalled a story she had read about the importance of the Legal Written Buyer Agreement. This vital document represented more than just paperwork—it marked the beginning of a true partnership with her real estate professional, Jake. Their agreement was rooted in mutual respect, transparency, and a shared commitment to her best interests.

"Let's take a moment to review a few key points about the Written Buyer Agreement," Jake said warmly as they settled into a cozy corner of the café, the scent of fresh coffee in the air. He knew that helping Sarah feel confident, they both had come to know and enjoy, and informed what was essential, starting the process on the right foot.

"Essentially, this agreement is a formal understanding between you and me," Jake explained. "It outlines the services I'll provide, as well as the terms of my compensation." He went on to explain that this requirement was introduced following the landmark National Association Settlement, effective November 26, 2024—a change designed to bring more fairness and transparency to the home-buying process.

As they delved deeper into the agreement, Jake outlined the significant benefits it would provide. "This document lays out the expectations you have for my services," he explained. "It also clearly specifies how I will be compensated. This clarity helps us establish a strong foundation for our working relationship, reducing potential confusion as we navigate your home search together."

Sarah nodded thoughtfully, realizing the significance of having everything spelled out. "So, when we start touring homes, I'll be asked to sign this agreement beforehand?"

"**Exactly!** Whether we meet in person or tour virtually, signing the agreement ensures we are on the same page moving forward," Jake confirmed. "However, if you're just visiting an open house or casually inquiring about services, a signature isn't immediately necessary."

With this newfound understanding, Sarah felt empowered. The Written Buyer Agreement not only reinforced her partnership with Jake but also provided a clear framework that would enhance communication and collaboration as they navigated the often-complex home-buying process.

Next Steps in the Home-Buying Journey: "Now that we've solidified your understanding of the Written Buyer Agreement," Jake continued, "let's review the steps involved in purchasing a home and some of the essential services I will provide along the way."

Together, they would embark on this journey, equipped with knowledge, clarity, and a strong commitment to making Sarah's dream of homeownership a reality.

Complete List of Major STEPS When Preparing to Purchase Home Select real estate professional: This may take some time, but you want someone with experience, a complete understanding of the new real estate industry, and who is committed to helping you find the home of your choice and negotiate the price that meets your needs.

Before you start looking at homes and lenders, there are several crucial steps you should take to ensure you're well-prepared for the home-buying process. Enter into communication with your selected Agent to determine what their involvement includes.

Assess Your Financial Situation:

- **Check Your Credit Score**: Obtain your credit report and score from all three major credit bureaus (Equifax, Experian, and Trans Union). Ensure there are no errors and work on improving your score if necessary.

- **Calculate Your Debt-to-Income Ratio (DTI)**: Lenders use your DTI ratio (it is in your best interest to keep your mortgage loan amount at 28% DTI) to determine your ability to repay the loan. According to the Federal Deposit Insurance Corp., lenders typically want the front-end ratio to be no more than 25% to 28% of your monthly gross income. The back-end ratio includes housing expenses plus long-term debt. Lenders prefer to see this number at 33% to 36% of your monthly gross income.

- **Establish Budget**: Use online calculators or consult with a financial advisor to figure out how much home you can afford based on your income, expenses, and savings.

Save for a Down Payment and Other Costs

Down Payment:

Save for a down payment, typically 20% of the home's purchase price, though some loans allow for lower percentages.

- Research if you are eligible for down payment assistance or closing

- Closing Costs: Save for closing costs, which have commonly been between 3-8% of the home's purchase price.

- Emergency Fund: Ensure you have an emergency fund to cover unexpected expenses.

Obtaining Mortgage Pre-Approval

- **Research Mortgage Options**: Understand different types of mortgages (fixed-rate, adjustable-rate, FHA, VA, USDA loans, or Credit Unions) and choose the best fit and the lender that charges the least amount of service fees for your situation.

- **Shop Around for Lenders**: Compare rates and terms of various lenders to find the best deal.

- **Gather Documentation**: Prepare necessary documents such as tax returns, pay stubs, bank statements, and identification. The Appendix contains a detailed list of all documents required for approval.)

- **Obtain the Pre-Approval Document**: Obtain a pre-approval letter from your chosen lender to show Sellers you're a serious Buyer with financing in place.

- **Provide a copy of the pre-approval letter to the Buyer's Agent.**

Note: While working in real estate for four decades, my experience has included success if a general letter to a Seller is composed, indicating that you truly feel that this will be your home forever, loving all that is included. Statistically, I had 100% success for every letter I wrote to Seller.

Define Your Home-Buying Criteria

- **Prioritize Your Needs and Wants**: Make a list of must-haves and nice-to-haves in a home (e.g., location, size, amenities, schools).

- **Neighborhoods research**: Look into neighborhoods that match your criteria and budget. Consider factors such as commute times, school quality, safety, and amenities.

Assemble Your Home-Buying Team

- **Hire Other Professionals**: Consult with your real estate Agent, whom you may assist when you need a real estate attorney, home inspector, or appraiser. Your Agent can recommend reliable professionals.

Preparing for the Search

- **Stay Organized**: Create a system to track the homes you view, your communications with your Agent, and any notes or preferences.

- **Be Ready to Act Quickly**: The housing market can move fast, so be prepared to make decisions and submit contracts promptly. Taking these steps will help you enter the home-buying process with confidence, ensuring you're financially prepared and have a clear understanding of your needs and options.

- **When seeking a home in your price range**, it is recommended to consider a variety of specific factors to ensure the property meets your needs and preferences.

Location - Identify Key aspects of home and location.

- **Neighborhood**: Safety, reputation, and overall vibe of the neighborhood.

- **Proximity to Work**: Commute times and ease of access to work or school.

- **Amenities**: Nearby facilities such as parks, shopping centers, restaurants, and public transportation.

- **Schools**: Quality of local schools is especially important for families with children.

Home Size and Layout

- **Square Footage**: Total living space and how it accommodates their needs.

- **Number of Bedrooms and Bathrooms**: Ensuring there are enough for the family size and future needs.

- **Floor Plan**: Preference for open vs. segmented spaces, flow between rooms, and layout suitability for their lifestyle.

Condition of the Home

- **Age of the Home**: Older homes may have more charm but might require more maintenance.

- **Maintenance and Upgrades**: Recent renovations, the condition of major systems (roof, HVAC, plumbing, electrical), and the quality of materials used.

- **Energy Efficiency**: Insulation, windows, and energy-efficient appliances that can reduce utility costs.

- **Outdoor Space**

- **Yard Size**: Space for children to play, gardening, or entertaining.

- **Privacy**: Fencing, distance from neighbors, and landscaping that provides seclusion.

- **Condition**: Maintenance level of the lawn, patio, and any outbuildings or structures like sheds or garages.

Future Potential

- **Room for Expansion**: Possibility to add additional rooms or building extensions in the future.

- **Resale Value**: Potential for property value appreciation over time-based on market trends and developments in the area.

Style and Aesthetics

- **Architectural Style**: Preference for certain types of architecture (modern, colonial, ranch, etc.).

- **Interior Design**: Features like flooring, countertops, cabinetry, and overall interior finishes.

Cost Considerations

Affordability:

- Ensure the home fits within the budget, considering mortgage payments, taxes, insurance, and maintenance costs.

- **Property Taxes**: Annual taxes and how they compare to similar homes in the area.

- **Homeowners Association (HOA) and (CDD) Community Development District Fees**: Any additional costs for community maintenance and amenities.

Inspection Results

- **Structural Integrity**: Ensuring there are no major issues with the foundation, roof, or overall structure.

- **Pest Inspections**: Checking for any signs of infestations or damage caused by pests.

- **Compliance with Codes**: Verifying that the home meets local building codes and standards (really important – not to be overlooked.)

New Regulations on Disclosure: What Sellers and Buyers Need to Know

In the ever-evolving realm of real estate, staying informed about disclosure requirements is crucial for anyone involved in the Buying and Selling process. With the recent regulatory changes stemming from the legal case of the Revolutionary Plaintiff vs. the National Association, Sellers must now navigate an updated landscape of obligations designed to foster transparency and protect all parties involved.

As Emily prepared to meet with her Client, Laura, who was looking to sell her property, she understood the weight of these new requirements. "It's essential for you to understand what needs to be disclosed to potential Buyers," Emily said as they sat at the kitchen table, reviewing the necessary steps.

Key New Disclosure Requirements

Within this new framework, Emily outlined the key disclosure requirements that Sellers must now adhere to:

- **Property Condition**: "You'll need to provide comprehensive information about the physical condition of your property," Emily explained. "This includes any defects or issues, such as foundational cracks or plumbing problems. Honesty here helps build trust with Buyers."

- **Insurance Claims**: "Any past insurance claims made on the property must also be disclosed," she added. "This can include anything from water damage repairs to roof replacements."

- **Neighborhood Nuisances**: Emily continued, "It's important to inform potential Buyers about any nuisances in the area, like noise from nearby businesses or upcoming zoning changes. Keeping Buyers informed helps manage their expectations and protects you in the long run."

- **Consequences of Non-Compliance:** Laura listened intently, realizing that compliance with these regulations was not merely a formality but a crucial component of the selling process.

Emily emphasized, "If you withhold critical information, you could face legal risks for misrepresentation or fraud. Additionally, regulatory bodies may impose fines, which could damage your reputation and finances."

Best Practices for Compliance

To ensure compliance with these new regulations, Emily recommended a few best practices:

- **Detailed Checklists**: "Using checklists can help you ensure that all new disclosure requirements are met," she advised. If checklists are unavailable, she offered to review the specific changes with Laura.

- **Templates**: "Utilizing templates for disclosure documents provided by real estate associations or legal professionals can simplify the process. It ensures you don't miss important details that need to be documented," Emily encouraged.

Impact on the Selling Process

Emily highlighted the broader implications these changes could have for the selling process. "While thorough inspections and detailed documentation might lengthen the time before closing, they significantly enhance transparency," she explained.

"Transparent disclosures foster trust with Buyers, streamline negotiations, and can even increase your property's appeal."

Practical Example:

As their conversation continued, Emily shared a real-life example for context. "Let's say you discover a sewer line issue during a Listing inspection," she noted. "If you address the repair and document the process, you can use this as a selling point to show that you're proactive and reliable. This not only ensures compliance with the new laws but also enhances the property's marketability."

While the new disclosure regulations introduce additional requirements for Sellers and the benefits of Buyers, they also elevate the standards of property transactions. By promoting fairness and transparency, these changes ultimately benefit both Sellers and Buyers alike. With this knowledge, Laura felt better prepared to face the market and understand the importance of compliance.

"Remember, if you have questions at any time during this process, don't hesitate to reach out to me," Emily reassured her. "As your Agent, I'm here to ensure you understand every step of the way. Your education and comfort are my top priorities."

Summary:

Empowerment through the Buyer-Agent Partnership

In the journey to homeownership, the role of the Buyer's Agent is crucial for navigating the complexities of the real estate market. As outlined in this chapter, the partnership between Buyers and their Agents is characterized by collaboration, transparency, and commitment to achieving the Buyer's goals.

The **Written Buyer Agreement** serves not only as a formal contract but as a declaration of trust and understanding between the Buyer and Agent. This agreement empowers Buyers by laying out the services the Agent will provide while clearly defining compensation structures. Armed with this knowledge, Buyers can approach the home-buying process with greater confidence and clarity.

Key aspects of working with a Buyer's Agent include:

- **Understanding Needs**: Agents take time to discuss preferences, priorities, and budget constraints to align property searches with Buyer goals.

- **Market Expertise**: Buyers benefit from Agents' insights on local market trends, which help them identify valuable opportunities.

- **Accessing Listings**: MLS resources ensure Buyers receive tailored property searches, opening doors to homes that meet their criteria.

- **Negotiation Support**: A skilled Agent will help negotiate terms, prices, and contingencies, advocating effectively for the Buyer's best interests.

- **Comprehensive Guidance**: From inspections to closing, Buyer's Agents offer advice and support throughout the purchasing journey

The changes resulting from the Revolutionary Plaintiffs' Settlement further enhance the relationship between Buyers and their Agents by emphasizing transparency and accountability. With Buyers now empowered with greater information, they have more control in negotiations and can make informed, strategic decisions at every step.

As you embark on your home-buying adventure, remember the importance of choosing a knowledgeable and committed Buyer's Agent. This partnership can significantly influence the success of your experience, ensuring that your needs are met while navigating potential challenges.

Equipped with insights from the Written Buyer Agreement and a strong advocate by your side, you are poised to make confident decisions in today's dynamic real estate market. Embrace the empowerment that comes with this partnership, and let it guide you toward fulfilling your dream of homeownership.

Complete List of Major Steps When Preparing to Purchase a Home

- **Embrace the Benefits:** The advantages are astounding. This agreement vividly delineates your expectations, clarifying the services your Agent will deliver while establishing how they will be compensated. Picture a mutual understanding blossoming that reduces confusion as you navigate toward your new abode.

- *But beware!* As you tour homes that capture your imagination, remember that signing the agreement is a rite of passage — one that solidifies your commitment to the journey ahead. Whether in person or through the glowing screen of a virtual tour, this agreement must be in place before you embark on inspections.

- **Who Should Sign?** Fear not if you're simply strolling through an open house or casually flirting with the idea of real estate—no immediate signature is required. The agreement comes into play once you decide to delve deeper, setting the stage for the next level of exploration.

- **The Financial Landscape:** Imagine your financial landscape lit by the warm glow of understanding. While you are responsible for compensating your Agent, it is essential to note that you are not limited—negotiate with confidence! You can discuss terms that may allow for compensation from the Seller or their Agent.

- **Flexibility in Relationships:** Dare to embrace the freedom this agreement gives you; it doesn't dictate a type of relationship with your Agent. Explore the opportunities that allow for diverse business arrangements tailored to your needs.

- **Changing the Narrative:** If circumstances dictate a shift in your agreement, fear not. You are granted the power to alter or exit the agreement with mutual consent, offering you the freedom to adapt as necessary. Just remember to read the terms thoroughly and engage in open conversations with your Agent.

With your real estate professional by your side, ready to navigate the exhilarating twists and turns of the home-buying process, envision the journey as one of collaboration, respect, and unwavering support. And should questions arise, fear not—your real estate professional is always eager to provide the clarity you seek.

Prepare yourself for an adventure that is both thrilling and rewarding, transforming your dream of homeownership into a breathtaking reality!

Conclusion

In conclusion, real estate professionals play a crucial role in facilitating property transactions by serving as knowledgeable guides and advocates. From navigating the complexities of the market to negotiating favorable terms, they ensure that Buyers and Sellers have the support and expertise necessary to make informed decisions. By understanding the importance of active communication regarding compensation and the necessity of clear agreements, Clients can foster a productive partnership with their Agents. Engaging in proactive discussions about financial arrangements and leveraging the new forms introduced by the Settlement empowers Clients to negotiate terms that best suit their needs. Ultimately, the relationship between a Buyer and their real estate professional is built on trust, transparency, and shared objectives.

Whether clients are navigating the intricate process of purchasing their first or second home or seeking to make a strategic investment, the guidance of a skilled real estate professional enhances their overall experience and contributes to successful outcomes. As homebuyers embark on their journey, embracing the insights and resources offered by real estate professionals ensures that they are well-equipped for the challenges ahead.

By making informed choices and utilizing the expertise of industry professionals, Buyers can confidently embark on their real estate journey, paving the way for a rewarding and beneficial experience in the market. Overall, the impact of the National Association Settlement on the real estate industry is overwhelming, leading to increased transparency, a shift in how compensations are negotiated, and a greater emphasis on ethical behavior. Real estate professionals will adapt to these changes by embracing new practices, enhancing their skills, and focusing on providing exceptional service to meet consumers' evolving expectations.

Written Buyer Agreement: As they delved deeper into the agreement, Jake outlined the significant benefits it would provide. "This document lays out the expectations you have for my services," he explained. "It also clearly specifies how I will be compensated. This clarity helps us establish a strong foundation for our working relationship, reducing potential confusion as we navigate your home search together."

Imagine embarking on an exciting adventure without a map. You know your destination, but without clear directions, you risk getting lost. The Written Buyer Agreement provides clarity and guidance throughout our journey the necessary Written Buyer Agreement," she explained, "as well as the options for negotiating your Buyer's Agent compensation." This openness laid the groundwork for a trusting partnership.

Real Estate Scale of Justice

In the realm where brick and dreams collide,
A challenge emerged, a fierce divide.
A couple of people, voices raised high,
Questioned the system, aiming to clarify.

With money shrouded in shadows and doubt,
They sought transparency to root it out.
Allegations of practices, unfair and concealed,
Their fight for the truth and their hopes were revealed.

Antitrust whispers in the air of the room,
Could change be on the rise, or were fears set to loom?
The lawyers stood firm, with fervor they spoke,
Against age-old systems, they challenged the cloak.

The ruling would mark a bold turning page,
Shaping the future of this vibrant stage.
For Buyer and Seller, a clarion call,
To understand pricing, their rights after all.

A shift in the landscape, a promise for fairness,
Where transparency blossoms and trust fills the air.
With lessons laid bare, and reforms in flight,
The case would inspire new paths in the light.

In a sunshine state and markets afar,
Justice in real estate shines bright like a star!

May Success be in your future!

MEW

161

List of Appendixes that Summarize and provide definitions of all key elements

Appendices

- **Appendix 1:** Settlement Compliance Essentials

- **Appendix 2:** Comprehensive List of Standardized Forms

- **Appendix 3:** Definitions for First-Time Buyers & Sellers

- **Appendix 4:** Key Definitions & Topics for All Buyers & Sellers

- **Appendix 5:** Seller Checklists

- **Appendix 6:** Real Estate Terms & Lingo

- **Appendix 7:** Required Documents for Lender Mortgage Approval

- **Appendix 8:** Key Areas of Change Affecting Real Estate Agents

- **Appendix 9:** Legal Challenges Faced by the National Association

Appendix 1: Settlement Compliance Essentials

Legal Definition of Compliance:

Compliance refers to the act of adhering to, and adherence to, laws, regulations, guidelines, and specifications relevant to an organization or specific field. In a business or organizational context (National Association) compliance involves ensuring that operations and practices meet legal and regulatory requirements, industry standards, and internal policies. Failure to comply can result in legal penalties, financial loss, and reputation damage.

- **Fair Housing Compliance Overview:** Permanently adhere to the Fair Housing Act, which prohibits discrimination based on race, color, religion, sex, national origin, familial status, and disability.

- **Fair Housing Compliance Action**: Regularly train staff on fair housing laws and maintain a policy that promotes diversity and non-discrimination in all real estate practices.

- **Fair Housing Compliance Disclosure Requirements**

- **Fair Housing Compliance Overview:** Permanently disclose all relevant property information to the Buyer, including but not limited to known defects, zoning issues, and neighborhood factors.

- **Action**: Implement permanent standard procedures to document disclosures and ensure that all required documentation is permanently shared with prospective Buyers and Sellers.

Advertising Regulations

- **Overview**: All advertising practices must permanently comply with federal and state laws, including the Truth in Advertising laws and guidelines from the Federal Trade Commission (FTC.)

- **Action**: ALWAYS review marketing materials to ensure accuracy and truthfulness and permanently avoid deceptive practices that could lead to legal claims.

Consumer Privacy Protection

- **Overview**: Permanently comply with laws related to consumer privacy, such as the General Data Protection Regulation (GDPR) for businesses that interact with EU (Europe) residents or California's Consumer Privacy Act (CCPA.)

- **Action**: Implement permanent strong data protection measures and clear privacy policies informing Clients about how their information is used and safeguarded.

Agency Disclosure

- **Overview**: Agents must clearly explain agency relationships to Clients, ensuring they understand whether you represent the Buyer, Seller, or both (Dual Agency.)

- **Action**: Use permanent written agreements and disclosures to clarify relationships and avoid confusion regarding representation.

Record Keeping

- **Overview**: Maintain accurate permanent records of all transactions, communication, and compliance documentation.

- **Action**: Develop a permanent document management system that allows for easy retrieval and organization of paperwork in case of audits or legal inquiries.

License Compliance

- **Overview**: Ensure that all real estate Agents and Brokers maintain their licenses and fulfill continuing education requirements.

- **Action**: Regularly verify license renewals and compliance with local real estate compensation requirements.

Although I have researched and worked on this manuscript, please remember I am not an attorney. Please do not hesitate to present legal questions to your local Real Estate Board the State Real Estate Association or a Real Estate Attorney.

Appendix 2: Comprehensive List of Standardized Forms

While the forms listed previously cover many of the primary and commonly used standardized forms provided by the National Association, there are indeed additional forms and variations that may also be included. Here is a more comprehensive overview of standardized forms commonly used in real estate transactions.

Listing Agreements:

- Exclusive Right to Sell Agreement

- Exclusive Agency Agreement

- Open Listing Agreement

- Net Listing Agreement

Purchase Agreements:

- Permanent **Written Buyer Agreement** NEW

- Residential Purchase Agreement

- Commercial Purchase Agreement

- Vacant Land Purchase Agreement

Disclosure Forms:

- Seller's Disclosure Notice

- Lead-Based Paint Disclosure

- Property Condition Disclosure

- Mold Disclosure

- Natural Hazards Disclosure

- Homeowners Association (HOA) Disclosures

Addendums and Amendments:

- Financing Addendum

- Inspection Addendum

- Contingency Addendum

- Amendment to Contract

Agency Disclosure Forms:

- Buyer Agency Agreement

- Dual Agency Disclosure Form

- Disclosure of Agency Relationships

Lease Agreements:

- Residential Lease Agreement

- Commercial Lease Agreement

- Lease Renewal Agreement

Counteroffers:

- Counteroffer Form Addendums

Closing Statements:

- Closing Disclosure

- Settlement Statement (HUD-1)

Referral Agreements:

- Broker Referral Agreement

- Agent Referral Agreement

Property Management Forms:

- Management Agreement

- Tenant Application

- Notice to Pay Rent or Quit

Tenant Forms:

- Lease Termination Notice

- Notice of Rent Increase

Miscellaneous Forms:

- Notice of Default

- Short Sale Addendum

- Home Inspection Report

- Loan Application Forms

Appendix 3 Definitions for First-Time Buyers/Sellers

- **First-Time Homebuyers Importance of Homeownership**: Understanding the benefits of owning a home, including financial investment, stability, personal freedom, and potential tax advantages.

- **First-Time Homebuyers Overview of the Buying/Selling Process**: A brief explanation of the steps involved from initial consideration to closing the transaction, highlighting key stages and decisions in the journey.

- **Creating a Budget and Gathering Documents for Lendor**: The process of outlining all expected income, expenses, and savings to establish a clear financial plan for purchasing or selling a home.

- **Research Lenders**: The act of comparing various mortgage lenders to find the best rates and loan products that align with the Buyer's financial situation.

- **Gathering Necessary Documentation**: Compiling essential financial documents like pay stubs, tax returns, and bank statements that lenders require for pre-approval.

- **Understanding Loan Options**: Familiarize oneself with different types of mortgage loans, such as fixed-rate, adjustable-rate, FHA loans, and VA loans, to make informed decisions.

- **Identifying Key Preferences and Must-Haves**: The process of determining specific features and amenities that the Buyer desires in a new home.

- **Staging and Marketing Your Property**: Preparing a home for sale through interior design and visual enhancements to attract potential Buyers, along with creating effective marketing strategies.

- **Navigating Offer Contingencies**: Understanding additional conditions included in an offer that must be met for the transaction to proceed, such as financing contingencies and home inspection contingencies.

- **Understanding Closing Documents**: Familiarize oneself with all documents involved in the closing process, including the deed, closing statement, and mortgage agreement.

- **Written Buyer Agreement:** This document lays out the expectations the Buyer has for Buyer's Agent services. It also clearly specifies how the Buyer's Agent will be compensated. This clarity helps Buyers establish a strong foundation for a working relationship, reducing potential confusion as the Buyer and Buyer's Agent navigate the home search together. The Written Buyer Agreement provides clarity and guidance, as well as negotiating the Buyer's Agent compensation.

Appendix 4 Definitions/topics for All Buyers/Sellers

- **Assessing Investment Returns and Market Position**: The practice of reviewing the financial performance of properties owned and strategizing for future transactions.

- **Conducting Comparative Market Analysis (CMA)**: A method applied by Agents to gauge the market value of a property by comparing it to similar properties sold in the area.

- **Crafting Win-Win Scenarios**: Finding solutions in negotiations that benefit both the Buyer and Seller, fostering a positive relationship and smoother transaction.

- **Evolving Real Estate Landscape**: Awareness of ongoing trends in the real estate market, including changes in consumer preferences, technology influences, and economic shifts.

- **Evaluating Additional Service Providers**: The act of selecting reliable contractors, inspectors, and other professionals necessary for the buying or selling process.

- **Evaluating Investment Potential**: The process of assessing a property's potential to generate returns, whether through appreciation, rental income, or tax advantages.

- **Staying Updated on Local and Federal Housing Laws**: Keeping informed about changes in legislation that affect real estate transactions, fair housing regulations, and consumer rights.

- **Understanding Disclosures and Contingencies**: Familiarity with the legal obligations to disclose property issues and the use of contingencies to protect one's interests in the transaction.

- **Understanding Seller Psychology**: Recognizing the motivations and emotional factors that influence a Seller's decisions during the negotiation process.

- **Utilizing Home Equity and Refinancing Options**: Understanding how to leverage accrued equity in a current home for financial benefits or to refinance existing mortgage terms.

Appendix 5: Real Estate Terms and Lingo

- **Agent/Broker Commission:** Compensation paid to the real estate Agents or Brokers for their services at closing.

- **Amortization Schedule**: A table detailing each periodic payment on a mortgage, showing the amount going towards principal and interest over the loan's lifetime. The lender can further explain if the Client's budget allows us to pay an additional amount per month, it will reduce the total mortgage payments. Don't miss out on this inquiry.

- **Appraisal: An evaluation performed by a licensed appraiser to determine the market value of the property. Lenders typically require an appraisal before approving a mortgage.**

- **Blockchain: (NEW)** A blockchain is a decentralized, distributed digital ledger that records transactions across many computers in such a way that the registered transactions cannot be altered retroactively. Each block in the chain contains several transactions, and every time a new transaction occurs on the blockchain, a record of that transaction is added to every participant's ledger. This system enhances security and transparency, as altering any piece of information would require changing all subsequent blocks, which is computationally impractical in large blockchain networks. Blockchains are foundational to cryptocurrencies such as BitCoin and have potential applications in various fields such as supply chain management, finance, and healthcare.

- **Closing**: The final step in a real estate transaction where the title is transferred from Seller to Buyer and all legal documents are signed and finalized.

- **Closing Costs**: Fees **associated with finalizing a real estate transaction, which could be influenced by new compensation models.**

- **Closing Disclosure**: A detailed accounting of a real estate transaction, including loan terms, projected monthly payments, and closing costs, presented to both Buyer and Seller before closing.

- **Contingency**: Conditions that must be met for a real estate contract to be binding (e.g., financing contingencies, inspection contingencies, appraisal contingencies).

- **Commission Split**: The division of compensation between the selling and buying Agents, crucial in the Sider-Burnett Verdict.

- **CRM (Customer Relationship Management)**: Software that manages interactions with Clients, a tool increasingly vital in a digitally driven marketplace.

- **Deed**: A legal document that transfers ownership of property from Seller to Buyer.

- **Earnest Money**: (Contract to Purchase Deposit) A deposit made by the Buyer to show serious intent to purchase, which is held in escrow and applied to the purchase price at closing.

- **Escrow Account**: Financial accounts where funds are held by a third party until specific conditions of the transaction, such as closing, are met. These funds are not released without appropriate signatures.

- **FSBO (For Sale by Owner)**: Indicates a property sale without Agent representation, a segment affected by changing the compensation dynamics.

- **Inspection Report**: A detailed document from a home inspector outlining the condition of a property, including any existing or potential issues.

- **Lead Generation**: The process of attracting and converting consumers/prospects, which may shift with new compensation strategies.

- **Metric**: Used by lenders to assess risk, comparing the loan amount to the appraised value of the property.

- **MLS (Multiple Listing Service)**: A database for real estate Listings, a critical tool for Agents that may see changes in usage or policies post-verdict.

- **Mortgage**: A **loan used to purchase real estate, where the property itself serves as collateral.**

- **Mortgage Note**: Legal Note/lending agreement issued by lender and signed by borrower(s). The Mortgage note outlines the loan and the borrower's signature promise to repay. If the Client is married, but if the loan is just using the husband or wife on the note application, at closing the deed will be in both names.

- **Notary**: An official who verifies the identities of the parties involved in the transaction and witnesses the signing of the documents.

- **Pre-Approval**: A lender's conditional agreement to loan a specific amount of money based on the assessment of the borrower's financial situation. Pre-approval requires that financial documents identified by the lender are submitted and all documents required are signed.

- **Principal**: The original sum of money borrowed on a mortgage loan, excluding interest.

- **ROI (Return on Investment)**: Reflects the performance of real estate investments, crucial in discussions about the financial implications of the Sider-Burnett verdict.

- **SEO (Search Engine Optimization** is A critical component of digital marketing for real estate, enhancing visibility in a competitive online space.

- **Settlement Statement**: A document that itemizes the finances of a real estate transaction, detailing fees, payments, and the amounts due to and from parties involved.

- **Title: A legal document identifying and** recording **the ownership of property.**

- **Title Insurance:** A policy that protects lenders and homeowners against claims or disputes over the ownership of the property, should mistakes be identified post-closing.

- **Title Search:** The process of examining public records to confirm a property's legal ownership and to ensure there are no claims or liens against it.

- **Underwriting**: To obtain a mortgage the lender must evaluate the borrower's risks. This includes credit checks, income verification, and much more.

- **Virtual Tours**: An increasingly popular tech tool for showcasing properties, reflecting the shift towards digital marketing.

- **1031 Exchange**: A real estate investment term that could be affected by how new compensation structures influence investment strategies.

Appendix 6 SELLER CHECKLISTS

Pre-Listing Activities

- Make an appointment with the Seller to present a Listing presentation,

- Send Seller a written or e-mail confirmation of the Listing appointment and call to confirm.

- Review pre-appointment questions,

- Research all comparable currently listed properties,

- Research "Average Days on Market" for this property of this type, price range, and location.

- Download and review property tax roll information,

- Prepare "Comparable Market Analysis" (CMA) to establish fair market value,

- Obtain a copy of the subdivision plat/complex layout,

- Research property ownership & deed type,

- Research the property's public record information for lot size & dimensions,

- Research and verify legal description,

- Research the property's land use coding and deed restrictions,

- Research property's current use and zoning,

- Verify legal names of owner(s) in the county's public property records,

- Prepare the Listing presentation package with the above materials,

- Perform exterior "Curb Appeal Assessment" of subject property,

- Compile and assemble formal files on a property,

- Confirm current public schools and explain the impact of schools on market value,

- Review the Listing appointment checklist to ensure all steps and actions have been completed Listing Appointment Presentation,

- Give Seller an overview of current market conditions and projections,

- Review of Agents and company's credentials and accomplishments in the market

- Present the company's profile and position or "niche" in the marketplace

- Present CMA Results to Seller, including Comparable, Sold, Current Listings & Expired

- Offer pricing strategy based on professional judgment and interpretation of current market conditions

- Discuss Goals With Seller To Market Effectively

- Explain the market power and benefits of Multiple Listing Service

- Explain the market power of web marketing, IDX, and REALTOR.com

- Explain the work the Brokerage and Agent do "behind the scenes" and the Agent's availability on weekends

- Explain the Agent's role in taking calls to screen for qualified Buyers and protect the Seller from curiosity seekers

- Present and discuss the strategic master marketing plan

- Explain different agency relationships and determine the Seller's preference

- Review and explain all clauses in the Listing Contract & Addendum and obtain the Seller's signature

Once the Property is Under the Listing Agreement

- Review current title information

- Measure overall and heated square footage

- Measure interior room sizes

- Confirm lot size via owner's copy of the certified survey, if available

- Note any unrecorded property lines, agreements, and easements

- Obtain house plans, if applicable and available

- Review house plans and make a copy

- Order plat map for retention in property's Listing file

- Prepare showing instructions for Buyers' Agents and agree on showing time window with Seller

- Obtain current mortgage loan(s) information: companies and loan account numbers

- Verify current loan information with lender(s)

- Check to determine whether loan(s) are assumable and any special requirements.

- Discuss possible Buyer financing alternatives and options with Seller

- Review current appraisal if available

- Identify the Homeowner Association manager, if applicable

- Verify Homeowner Association Fees with the manager - mandatory or optional and current annual fee

- Order copy of the Homeowner Association bylaws, if applicable

- Research electricity availability and the supplier's name and phone number

- Calculate average utility usage from the last 12 months of bills

- Research and verify the city sewer/septic tank system

- Water System: Calculate average water fees or rates from the last 12 months of bills)

- Well Water: Confirm well status, depth, and output from the Well Report

- Natural Gas: Research/verify availability and supplier's name and phone number

- Verify security system, current term of service, and whether owned or leased.

- Verify if Seller has a transferable Termite Bond

- Ascertain the need for lead-based paint disclosure

- Prepare a detailed list of property amenities and assess the market impact

- Prepare a detailed list of the property's "Inclusions & Conveyances with Sale'

- Compile a list of complete repairs and maintenance items

- Send "Vacancy Checklist" to the Seller if the property is vacant

- Explain the benefits of the Homeowner Warranty to Seller

- Assist Sellers with the completion and submission of the Homeowner Warranty Application

- When received, place the Homeowner Warranty in the property file for conveyance at the time of sale

- Verify if the property has rental units involved. And if so:

- Make copies of all leases for retention in the Listing file

- Verify all rents & deposits

- Inform tenants of the Listing and discuss how showings will be handled

- Arrange for the installation of yard sign

- Assist Seller with completion of Seller's Disclosure form

- "New Listing Checklist" Completed

- Review results of the Curb Appeal Assessment with the Seller and provide suggestions to improve salability.

- Review results of Interior Décor Assessment and suggest changes to shorten time on the market.

- Load Listing into Transaction Management Software Program

Entering Property in MLS Checklist

- Prepare MLS Profile Sheet — The Agent is responsible for "quality control" and accuracy of Listing data and payment amounts are prohibited permanently from being entered into ML.

- Enter property data from the Profile Sheet into the MLS Listing Database

- Proofread MLS database Listing for accuracy - including proper placement in the mapping function

- Add property to the company's Active Listings list

- Provide Seller with signed copies of Listing Agreement and MLS

- Profile Sheet Data Form within 48 hours

- Take additional photos for uploading into MLS and use them in flyers. Discuss the efficacy of panoramic photography in Marketing the Listing,

- Create print and Internet ads with Seller's input; Coordinate showings with owners, tenants, and other real estate professionals; all calls will be addressed - weekends included,

- Install electronic lock box if authorized by owner. Program with agreed-upon showing time windows,

- Prepare mailing and contact list and review with the Client for approval,

- If approved, generate mail-merge letters to the contact list; Create "Just Listed" labels & reports,

- Review comparable MLS Listings regularly to ensure property remains competitive in price, terms, conditions, and availability.

- Prepare property marketing brochure for Seller's review,

- Arrange for printing or copying of the supply of marketing brochures or fliers,

- Upload Listing to the company and Agent Internet site,

- Mail Out "Just Listed" notice to neighborhood residents,

- Advise Network Referral Program of Listing,

- Provide marketing data to Buyers coming through international relocation networks,

- Provide marketing data to Buyers coming from referral networks,

- Provide "Special Feature" cards for marketing, if applicable.

- Submit ads to companies participating in the Internet real estate sites,

- Price changes are conveyed promptly to all Internet groups,

- Reprint/supply brochures promptly as needed,

- Loan information reviewed and updated in MLS as required,

- Feedback e-mails/faxes sent to Buyers' Agents after showings

- Review weekly Market Study,

- Discuss feedback from Agents with the Seller to determine if changes will accelerate the sale,

- Place regular weekly update calls to Seller to discuss marketing & pricing,

- Promptly enter price changes in the MLS Listing database.

- Receive and review all offers to purchase contracts submitted by Buyers or Buyers' Agent,

- Evaluate offer(s) and area and prepare a "net sheet" on each for the owner for comparison purposes (Net Sheets are different in each state because they reflect as many closings cost expenses as possible that have been revealed,

- Counsel Seller on offers. Explain the merits and weaknesses of each component of each offer,

- Contact Buyers' Agents to review Buyer's qualifications and discuss the offer,

- Fax/email or deliver Seller's Disclosure to Buyer's Agent or Buyer upon request and before offer if possible,

- Confirm the Buyer is pre-qualified by calling the Loan Officer (Sellers and Real Estate Professionals have a great advantage of success if the Loan Officer provides a pre-qualified form. This reflects that the Lender has all the documents needed to approve the Buyer.)

- Negotiate all offers on Seller's behalf, setting a time limit for a loan, loan approval and loan closing date,

- Prepare and convey any counteroffers, acceptance, or amendments to Buyer's Agent,

- Fax copies or email contract and all addendums to the closing attorney or title company,

- When the Offer to Purchase Contract is accepted, signed by Seller, delivered to Buyer's Agent,

- Record and promptly deposit the Buyer's earnest money in an escrow account,

- Disseminate "Under-Contract Showing Restrictions" if Seller requests,

- Deliver copies of the fully signed Contract to Purchase to Seller

- Fax/deliver copies of the Offer to Purchase contract to the Selling Agent

- Fax copies of the Offer to Purchase contract to the lender,

- Provide copies of the signed Offer to Purchase contract for office file,

- Advise Seller in handling additional offers to purchase submitted between contract and closing,

Change status in MLS to "Sale Pending",

- Update transaction management program to show "Sale Pending",

- Review Buyer's credit report results -- Advise Seller of worst- and best-case scenarios,

- Provide credit report information to the Seller if the property will be Seller-financed.

- Assist Buyer with obtaining financing, if applicable, and follow up as necessary,

- Coordinate with lender on Discount Points being locked in with dates,

- Deliver unrecorded property information to the Buyer,

- Order septic system inspection, if applicable,

- Receive and review septic system reports and assess any possible impact on sales,

- Deliver a copy of the septic system inspection report to the lender & Buyer,

- Deliver Well Flow Test Report copies to Lender & Buyer and property Listing file,

- Verify mold inspection ordered if required.

- Confirm Verifications of Deposit & Buyer's Employment Have Been Returned,

- Follow Loan Processing Through To The Underwriter,

- Add lender and other vendors to transaction management program so Agents, Buyers, and Seller can track the progress of sales,

- Contact the lender weekly to ensure processing is on track,

- Relay final approval of Buyer's loan application to Seller.

Home Inspection

- Coordinate Buyer's professional home inspection with Seller,

- Review of the home inspector's report,

- Enter completion into transaction management tracking software program,

- Explain the Seller's responsibilities concerning loan limits and interpret any clauses in the contract,

- Ensure Seller's compliance with Home Inspection Clause requirements,

- Recommend or assist Seller with identifying and negotiating with trustworthy contractors to perform any required repairs,

- Negotiate payment and oversee completion of all required repairs on Seller's behalf.

The Appraisal

- Schedule Appraisal,

- Follow-Up On Appraisal,

- Enter completion into transaction management program,

- Assist Seller in questioning appraisal report if it seems too low,

- Provide comparable sales in market pricing for Closing Preparations and Duties,

- Contract Is Signed by All Parties. Coordinate closing process with Buyer's Agent and Lender,

Update closing forms & files,

- Ensure all parties have all the forms and information needed to close the sale,

- Select the location where closing will be held,

- Confirm closing date and time and notify all parties,

- Assist in solving any title problems (boundary disputes, easements, etc.) or in obtaining Death Certificates,

- Work with Buyer's Agent: schedule and conduct Final Walk-Thru before closing.

- Research all tax, HOA, utility, and other applicable proration,

- Request final closing figures from closing Agent (attorney or title company),

- Receive & carefully review closing figures to ensure accuracy of preparation,

- Forward verified closing figures to the Buyer's Agent,

- Request copy of closing documents from closing Agent,

- Confirm Buyer and Buyer's Agent have received the title insurance commitment,

- Provide "Homeowners Warranty" for availability at closing,

- Review all closing documents carefully for errors. Forward closing documents to Absentee Seller as requested,

- Review documents with the closing Agent (attorney),

- Provide earnest money deposit (by transfer bank to bank. Closing agents do not accept cash or Certified Checks.) check from escrow account to closing Agent

- Coordinate this closing with Seller's next purchase and resolve any timing problems,

- Have a "no surprises" closing so that the Seller receives net proceeds check at closing,

- Refer Sellers to one of the best Agents at their destination, if applicable,

- Change MLS status to Sold. Enter the sale date, price, selling Broker and Agent's ID numbers, etc.,

- Closeout Listing in transaction management program Follow-Up After Closing,

- Answer questions   about filing claims with the Homeowner Warranty company if requested.

- Attempt to clarify and resolve any conflicts about repairs if the Buyer is not satisfied.

- Respond to any follow-up calls and provide any additional information required from office files,

- Mark the First Anniversary sale date to send the Client a congratulations note.

Appendix 7: Documents Required by Lender for Mortgage Approval

Sample Lender/Mortgage Application documents required

Please remember: All documents must include the borrower's name, account number, bank information, and all pages of documents required.

- Enlarged copy of front and back of driver's license or State Issued ID

- W-2s and 1099's for the past 2 years, Social Security award letter if receiving income.

- Pay Stubs for the past 3 full months including year-to-date income.

- Most recent consecutive 2 months bank, checking, savings, and investment statements for checking, savings, and investment accounts including applicant's name, account #, Bank Institution, and all pages in the statement

- Documentation for any large non-payroll deposits.

Application to Purchase

- A deposit to purchase must be made when the contract has been signed and agreed upon by all parties.

- Purchase contract, signed by all parties, when purchasing a home.

- Documentation of any earnest payments and company who received the deposit.

- Name and phone number of selected homeowner insurance Agent and Flood Insurance

- If applicable, provide a divorce decree and Friend of the Court Support order

- If a Veteran, please include DD214, Certification of Eligibility, verification of retirement benefits if applicable, and National Guard or Reservist statement if applicable.

- If working with a Veteran who is 100% disabled, research if they are required to pay property taxes annually.

- Copies of signed Federal income tax returns for the previous 2 years, including all schedules.

- If the rental property is owned, include a Copy of all leases, a Copy of mortgage statement(s), and Insurance and property tax statements.

- Copies of signed business Federal income tax returns for the last two years including all schedules and 1099's if applicable.

APPENDIX 8 Key areas of Settlement changes

The National Association **Settlement** and the changes it has mandated have had a significant impact on real estate practice. Here are some key areas of change that directly affect how real estate professionals must operate within the industry:

Greater Transparency in Transactions

- **Impact**: Real estate professionals are now required to disclose more information about compensation structures and fees. This includes the development of negotiation training to assist them in reaching a decision that all agree upon.

- **Practice Change:** Some resources identify 179 tasks that an Agent performs as well as a resource that identifies an additional 105 tasks necessary to bring the contract to close. (Please note that both of these resources can be found on the website.)

Changes in Commission Negotiation

- **Impact:** The **Settlement** has led to shifts in how compensations are discussed and negotiated between Agents and their Clients, as well as between cooperating Agents. Again, conversations may be more successful if negotiation is employed when needed.

- **Practice Change**: Agents may need to be more flexible and transparent in their compensation discussions, seeking to negotiate their rates and possibly offer alternative pricing structures. Again, some resources justify a real estate professional's rate or pricing structure

Increased Focus on Ethical Practices

- **Impact**: The **Self-Regulation** has underscored the importance of ethical behavior in real estate transactions.

- **Practice Change**: Real estate professionals are likely to see a renewed emphasis on ethics training, adherence to local and national guidelines, and promoting fair practices within their firms.

Impact on MLS Operations

- **Impact**: MLS systems have begun adjusting their policies to comply with the **Settlement**, leading to changes in how Listing information is shared and accessed.

- **Practice Change**: Real estate professionals may need to adapt to new MLS rules and procedures, including enhanced access for consumers and potential changes in how Listings are displayed.

Empowerment of Consumers

- **Impact**: Increased access to information gives consumers more power in the buying and selling process.

- **Practice Change**: Agents may need to adjust their strategies to account for more informed Clients who are better equipped to challenge traditional practices or negotiate terms on their own.

Emergence of Alternative Business Models

- **Impact**: The **Settlement** has opened the door for alternative Brokerage models, such as low-cost Brokerages and technology-based platforms that offer minimal services.

- **Practice Change**: Traditional Brokers may need to compete differently, potentially adopting service models that offer more flexibility or lower costs to attract Clients.

Education and Training Requirements

- **Impact**: The evolving landscape encourages real estate Agents to continue to educate themselves about negotiation, new regulations, and best practices. (The author will be providing educational resources for Negotiation.)

- **Practice Change**: Ongoing professional development and training will become crucial to staying compliant and competitive in the market.

Enhanced Marketing Strategies

- **Impact**: With consumers having direct access to more property information, Agents must refine their marketing strategies.

- **Practice Change**: Marketing may need to become more educational, providing value and insight rather than just advertising Listings.

Increased Accountability

- **Impact**: The **Settlement** has introduced a level of scrutiny and accountability in real estate transactions, pushing for compliance with the new regulations.

- **Practice Change**: Agents may have to implement measures to document their practices meticulously and ensure that they adhere to the new standards.

Focus on Client-Centered Approaches

- **Impact**: As Clients become more knowledgeable and empowered by the available information, real estate professionals must shift to a more Client-centered approach.

- **Practice Change: Agents** will likely need to take more time to listen to Clients' needs, offer tailored advice, and build stronger relationships based on trust and collaboration.

Appendix 9 Legal Challenges Faced by the National Association

The National Association has faced various legal issues over the years, ranging from antitrust concerns to allegations of discriminatory practices. Here are some key legal issues that have affected the organization:

Antitrust Violations: The National Association has been accused of engaging in anticompetitive practices, particularly related to its policies on access to Multiple Listing Services (MLS.) These allegations typically revolve around restrictions on access to MLS data and rules governing the use of lockboxes, which can limit competition among real estate professionals.

- **Class Action Lawsuits**: NAR has faced multiple class action lawsuits alleging antitrust violations. These lawsuits often involve allegations that the National Association's policies restrict competition among real estate professionals and drive-up compensation rates for consumers.

- **Discrimination Allegations**: The National Association has faced allegations of discriminatory practices, including steering Buyers or tenants to or away from certain neighborhoods based on race or other protected characteristics. These allegations have led to legal challenges and the **Settlement** aimed at promoting fair housing practices within the real estate industry.

- **Brokerage Regulation**: The National Association's policies and practices have also come under scrutiny from regulators and lawmakers concerned about potential conflicts of interest and consumer protection issues within the real estate Brokerage industry. This has led to increased regulatory oversight and calls for reforms to promote transparency and accountability.

• **Data Privacy and Security**: With the increasing use of technology in the real estate industry, the National Association has faced challenges related to data privacy and security. This includes concerns about the collection, use, and protection of sensitive consumer information, as well as compliance with data protection laws and regulations.

• **License Misconduct**: The National Association has had to address instances of misconduct or unethical behavior among its members, including violations of the association's code of ethics and professional standards. In some cases, these issues have resulted in legal actions and disciplinary proceedings against individual real estate Agents or Brokers.

These legal issues highlight the complex regulatory landscape and the ongoing challenges faced by the National Association and its members in the real estate industry. Addressing these issues often requires a combination of legal advocacy, policy reforms, and enhanced professional standards and practices within the industry.

Conclusion

Overall, the impact of the National Association **Settlement** on real estate practice is overwhelming, leading to increased transparency, a shift in the way compensations are negotiated, and a greater emphasis on ethical behavior. Real estate professionals will need to adapt to these changes by embracing new practices, enhancing their skills, and focusing on providing exceptional service to meet the evolving expectations of consumers. Please do not hesitate to present questions to your local Board, your State Association, or the National.

About the Author

To introduce myself (with a nickname of Molly), I am an accomplished real estate professional with a passion for helping individuals and families achieve their dreams of homeownership. My journey in the real estate industry began while I was still in college, when I made a significant investment by purchasing a four-family home. This venture provided a cost-effective living arrangement and established a lifelong commitment to real estate.

Over the years, working with my partner who also became a licensed real estate professional, expanded our portfolio by acquiring several properties, including a five-family home strategically located near a commuter train station, as well as two two-family homes we restored for tenants. As we approached retirement, we successfully invested in Florida real estate, embracing opportunities to grow our assets. However, we ultimately decided that retirement should be tenant-free, prompting me to transition into becoming a licensed Real Estate Agent, a Home Buyer Educator, and a licensed Broker working as a broker Agent.

My commitment to education and community empowerment is evident in the extensive list of qualifications I achieved. A proud member of the National Association of Realtors (NAR), I hold numerous designations, including Accredited Buyers Representative, Certified International Property Specialist, and Certified Residential Specialist, among others I have also made significant contributions to affordable housing through my education and work with national NeighborWorks.

Unprecedented Step-By-Step Real Estate Guide

As I established my goal, I focused on first-time homebuyers and have dedicated decades to counseling and educating new homeowners. My commitment to the industry has successfully helped over 100 individuals on a journey that resulted in first-time Buyers accomplishing their dream of owning a home, while also teaching First-Time Homebuyer classes in both Collier and Lee Counties in Florida. My efforts extended beyond traditional practices, and my goal expanded to embrace innovative solutions to empower real estate professionals and Clients.

While working continuously as a real estate professional, I was at the forefront of recent changes in the real estate landscape, particularly following the landmark Settlement initiated by the National Association of Realtors on November 26, 2024. In response to this pivotal moment, I wrote and published in 2025 my book titled: "UNPRECEDENTED Step-by-Step REAL ESTATE GUIDE: Essential Tools for Thriving in Today's Real Estate Market." This resource aims to guide Buyers, Sellers, and real estate professionals through the new dynamics of the market.

Additionally, I offer online classes designed to address industry changes, featuring topics such as negotiation strategies for Buyers and Sellers, transparency in transactions, and effectively utilizing ChatGPT to educate consumers about recent developments in real estate practices. With vast experience, numerous certifications, and dedication to fostering financial literacy and homeownership, my goal is to continue to be a respected figure in the real estate community. My unwavering commitment to my Clients and the industry exemplifies my belief that everyone deserves the opportunity to own a home and build a successful future.

Education and Achievements

National Association
Accredited Buyers Representative
Certified International Property Specialist
Certified Residential Specialist
Green Specialist
Graduate Real Estate Institute
Senior Real Estate Specialist
At Home With Diversity
Resort and 2nd home Property Specialist
Short Sale and Foreclosure Resource

Accomplishments through National Affordable Housing And Neighborworks
Advanced Evaluations of Affordable Housing
Affordable Housing Committee
Attainable Affordable Housing Workgroup
Center for Home Ownership and Counselling
Certification in Housing Counseling
Community of Real Estate Excellence
Financial Fitness: Teaching Financial Management Skills
Homebuyer Education Methods: Accelerated Training at the
Neighborworks Training Institute Chicago IL
Internet and Computing Core Certification
Neighborworks America
Prepurchase in Home Ownership Education
Real Estate Opportunity Best Practices

Microsoft
Database Administrator
Technical Education Instructor
Master Instructor Microsoft Office
Microsoft Certified Trainer

USDA
FHA's Loss Mitigation Training

IC3 Authorized Program Instructor:
- Internet and Computing Core Certification
  - Computing Fundamentals
- Key Applications and Living Online

Florida Housing Finance Corporation
Affordable Housing Solutions
REO Default Certified Professional

www.ingramcontent.com/pod-product-compliance
Lightning Source LLC
Chambersburg PA
CBHW041006210326
41597CB00006B/146